Plays for Y

Methuen Drama's *Plays for Young* ... selection of single plays and anth... perform. The series features the h... playwrights, which is age-approp... to help teachers and youth theatre leaders select the most suitable work for their group.

BY THE SAME AUTHOR

The Year of the Monkey and Other Plays
Easy Access for the Boys and All Over Lovely
Why Is John Lennon Wearing A Skirt?: Adult Child/
Dead Child and Other Stand-up Theatre Plays

Upfront Theatre

Why Is John Lennon Wearing A Skirt?
(**Stage2** version, large cast)

Arsehammers
(**Stage2** version, large cast)

The Year of the Monkey
(**Stage2** version, large cast)

Hard Working Families
(Original version, large cast)

CLAIRE DOWIE

Bloomsbury Methuen Drama
An imprint of Bloomsbury Publishing Plc

B L O O M S B U R Y
LONDON · OXFORD · NEW YORK · NEW DELHI · SYDNEY

Bloomsbury Methuen Drama

An imprint of Bloomsbury Publishing Plc

50 Bedford Square	1385 Broadway
London	New York
WC1B 3DP	NY 10018
UK	USA

www.bloomsbury.com

Bloomsbury is a registered trade mark of Bloomsbury Publishing Plc

This collection first published 2017

Introduction © Claire Dowie 2017

Why Is John Lennon Wearing a Skirt? (**Stage2** version, large cast)
© Claire Dowie, 2017
Arsehammers (**Stage2** version, large cast) © Claire Dowie, 2017
The Year of the Monkey (**Stage2** version, large cast) © Claire Dowie, 2017
Hard Working Families © Claire Dowie, 2017

Claire Dowie has asserted her right under the Copyright, Designs and Patents Act,
1988, to be identified as author of this work.

British Library Cataloguing-in-Publication Data
A catalogue record for this book is available from the British Library.

ISBN:	PB:	978-1-3500-1114-4
	ePub:	978-1-3500-1116-8
	ePDF:	978-1-3500-1115-1

Library of Congress Cataloging-in-Publication Data
A catalog record for this book is available from the Library of Congress.

Typeset by RefineCatch Limited, Bungay, Suffolk
Printed and bound in India

Contents

Introduction

I believe stand-up theatre is an art form most accessible to people, young and old, because it's less about art and more about life, and we've all lived one of those.

It mainly requires the confidence to stand on a stage, face the audience and deliver lines like a comedian. There is 'acting' involved if you want to do that, but if you believe in the character and the story you won't need the talent of a Dench or a McKellen. In fact the talent of a Dench or a McKellen can sometimes get in the way.

What you *will* need is a sense of humour, humanity and energy, and a desire not to bore or ignore an audience.

Which is why these plays are so perfect for young people.

Young people are still exploring life, learning about life, experimenting with feelings, sympathies, empathies, ways of working, ways of performing, and the last thing they are thinking is that their feet are stuck in mud, their heads are buried in sand or their hearts are set in stone. And though they may think they know everything about everything, they never think nothing can change.

Not that I wrote these plays with young people in mind.

I wrote these plays with me in mind.

When I switched from stand-up comedy to my own brand of stand-up theatre I needed something to perform. And since there was nothing till I wrote something, I wrote *Adult Child/Dead Child* (in the volume: *Why is John Lennon Wearing a Skirt? and other stand-up theatre plays*). I performed it as a solo piece all over the UK and Ireland and then other people asked if they could perform it too, giving a first inkling of young interest. Many people have performed that play solo, in twos and threes and more, in schools and theatres, amateur and professional, in the UK and round the world. At one point it was even banned for overuse as an audition piece. This was the first of my plays to be adapted by Liz Light for **Stage2**.

And so began a long, fruitful, mutually creative and enjoyable relationship and friendship, and I was proud to be asked, along with my longstanding director and producer, Colin Watkeys, to be a patron of **Stage2**.

Why is John Lennon Wearing a Skirt?, *Arsehammers*, and *Year of the Monkey* were originally solo shows and remain in print in that format. But the genius that is Liz Light also adapted them for **Stage2** and a huge cast. This seemed right and natural and added a dimension that I, as a solo performer, couldn't provide, and a feeling that others might want the benefit of large cast scripts. Hence this anthology.

Watching **Stage2** is a joy. Working with them is a gift, and Liz Light does a brilliant job. They speak individually and collectively of optimism, cooperation and belief and can make older people think twice. Feeling out of step and marginalized is not an age thing it's a universal thing, and the anxieties that are created in childhood can often cling into adulthood, creating a bond between young and old. The joy of **Stage2** and the joy of youth is the belief that things can change, things can improve, things can be made better. And this, I hope, is at the heart of all my writing.

Which brings us to *Hard Working Families* and the reason I wrote it specifically for **Stage2** and a large cast.

Hard Working Families is about young, older and even older people living together, trying together, crying together and fighting together in spite of obstacles, in spite of politics, in spite of false hopes, false goals and false ambition, in spite of life getting in the way. We all need each other, we all want each other and it's not about jobs or money or appearances or the class system or politics or ambition or even aspiration.

It's about biscuits.

Claire Dowie 2016

Why is John Lennon Wearing a Skirt?

Adapted by Liz Light

This version of *Why Is John Lennon Wearing A Skirt?* was first produced by **Stage2** at the Crescent Theatre, Birmingham, on 17 April 2014 with the following cast and creatives:

Young Johns: Primary School Age

Ellie Waide (**Y1**)   Izzy Cremins (**Y2**)

Violette Sprigg (**Y3**)   Emily Cremins (**Y4**)

Middle Johns: Secondary School Age

Laura Dowsett (**M1**)   Phoebe Stephenson (**M2**)

Emily Hawtin (**M3**)   Teigan Jones (**M4**)

Alice Nott (**M5**)   Meg Luesley (**M6**)

Old Johns: Work Place Age

Chloe Jennings (**O1**)   Sarah Middlemiss (**O2**)

Annabel Butcher (**O3**)   Rosie Nisbet (**O4**)

Mum	Helen Carter
Dad	Connor Fox
Friends	Isabella Jones-Rigby (**F1**)
	Goldie Mutta (**F2**)
	Sophia Adilypour (**F3**)
Girly Girls	Brianna Whitty (**G1**)
	Kloe Vincent (**G2**)
	Hanifa Ali (**G3**)
	Toni Earle-Randell (**G4**)
	Georgia Homer (**G5**)
	Hana Ali (**G6**)
Boyfriends	Dillan McKeever (**B1**)
	Bradley Layton (**B2**)
	Toby Jowitt (**B3**)
	Jack Deakin (**B4**)
	Alex Earle (**B5**)
	Mark James (**B6**)
	Robert Fretwell (**B7**)
	Dante Crawford (**B8**)
	Chris Beacham (**B9**)
	Gabriel Hudson (**B10**)

| **Nasty Teacher** | Aldora Lekgegaj |
| **Cookery Teacher** | Ana Pettifer |

| **Mum on Bus** | Maddie Adkins |
| **Girl on Bus** | Georgie Nott |

Careers Officer	Radelina Ancheva
Mr Banks	Dan Nash
Personnel Officer	Alex Earle

Chorus

Primo Agnello	Oliver Hanley	Connor Pollet
Sylvie Agnello	George Hannigan	Bella Quirin
Bianca Alecu	LaTia Harding	Shaqkeel Rahman
Tom Barber	Ella Harte	Sid Rao
Alex Barton	Lauren Harte	Jessica Ryan
Byron Creavin-Jerwood	Amber Harvey	Layla Shafiq
Khalid Daley	Reuben Jones-Rigby	Charlie Stewart
Annie Delaney	Simrat Kaur	Maddi Stewart
Louis Delaney	Daniel McCloskey	Ellie Swarbrick
Jonathan Dowsett	Alex McDonald	Sebastian Watkins
Priya Edwards	Kiah McPherson	Emma Watson
Alice Fenton	Siah Meadows	Daisy Wilkes
Tia Forbes	Mariam N'Dong	Finlay Yilmaz

Band
Keyboards Charlie Reilly
Drums Alex Earle
Lead Guitar Mark James
Bass Guitar George Mee
Backing Singers Ella Otomewo, Jacob Otomewo

Crew
Director Liz Light
Production Manager/Lighting Designer Chris Cuthbert
Technical Leader Jake Hotchin
Musical Director/Lines Allocations Charlie Reilly
Assistant Director Sarah Kemp
Production Assistant/Stage Manager Andrew Brown

Costume Assistant/Stage Manager Wallis Allen
Lighting Operator Ethan Tarr
Sound Operator Ewan Aldridge
Technical Assistant James Fenton
Backstage Manager Alex Pugh
Head Chaperone Lucy Bailey-Wright

Set
Brightly coloured, multilayered set with platforms and stairs. Band visible onstage the entire time. Moveable items e.g. blocks to denote different locations.

Music
Excerpts of Beatles' songs throughout.

Costume
All 'Johns' white shirts and grey skirts with school ties. All other characters brightly coloured as relevant e.g. Mum and 'Girls' in pink!

Characters

Young Johns: Primary School Age
Middle Johns: Secondary School Age
Old Johns: Work Place Age
Mum
Dad
Friends
Girly Girls
Boyfriends
Nasty Teacher
Cookery Teacher
Mum on Bus
Girl on Bus
Careers Officer
Mr Banks
Personnel Officer

Intro

M1   This was me at fourteen.

M2   I liked being fourteen,

M3   fourteen was a great age to be.

M4   I could be really grown up

M5   or really childish

M4   depending on what mood I was in . . .

M6   and I was really moody – well, according to my mum I was.

Mum   You're so moody, you are.

M1   Well, what do you expect Mum? I'm only fourteen

M2   it's my hormones – whatever they are.

M5   Mostly I suppose I was childish but I didn't care,

M3   I had three best friends, all tomboys,

Friends enter

M4   and we went round in a gang.

M6   The Fab Four we were known as:

G1, G2, G3   Here they come, the Fab Four,

G4, G5, G6   Watch out, it's the Fab Four.

M4, F1, F2, F3   That was us.

M1   'Course we started it, we called ourselves the Fab Four first because no one else would.

M4, F1, F2, F3   Call us the Fab Four.

G1   No, I don't want to.

M4, F1, F2, F3   Ah, go on,

G4   I don't want to.

M4, F1, F2, F3   Call us the Fab Four.

G1 – G6   Alright, you're the Fab Four, now bog off will ya!

MUSIC: 'Twist and Shout.'

Knicker Factor

M4   Secretly I named my friends Paul, George and Ringo, but I never told them (I'm not stupid), they just seemed to act like Paul, George and Ringo and that was good enough for me.

M1   I was John, of course, although you wouldn't think so to look at me dressed like this – but what could you do, it was compulsory, a school rule. Had its compensations though,

M5   like this tie for instance.

M1   Loved this tie, it was the first thing I put on in the morning, got up, put my tie on – mind you, it took me half an hour to get my shirt on but . . . when else could you wear a tie without having to answer awkward questions? I wore mine like that though (*Adjusts tie to untidy angle.*) sort of roguish –

M5   clever but dishevelled –

M1   a very Johnish look I thought. So I was quite happy with the top half of me, quite liked the top half of me.

M2   The bottom half I hated. Five days a week for five years I had to wear this thing and five days a week for five years I wanted to know why, what for, what was the point? A piece of material hanging round your waist. I mean, what could you do in it?

F1   Could you play football?

Trying to play while keeping skirt down.

M1–6   Yes, but you had to watch your knickers.

F2   Could you dive off your desk onto somebody's back and roll around the floor tussling?

M1–6   Yes, but you had to watch your knickers.

F3   Could you slump in your chair, bored and rebellious like James Dean?

M1–6   Yes, but you had to watch your knickers.

M4   You always had to watch your knickers.

M5   And of course you got the boys watching your knickers for you –

Chorus Boy   (*pulls up* **M5** *skirt*) 'whooo!'

M3   The knicker factor I called it. Why was it compulsory, a school rule to implement the knicker factor? Why couldn't we wear long ones down to the ankles, all sewn up, covered up and protected like the boys? Took all four of us and a lot of fighting to catch a glimpse of a boy's knickers – two on the arms, one sitting on the feet and one to pull down the trousers – and it was a lot more fun.

M6   I wouldn't have minded if we'd worn short ones, sort of semi-protected, in fact I did that once in needlework, instead of making an oven mitt, sewed it straight up the middle. Felt good, felt really clever, but I got told to stop it, got told to unpick it, got told,

Nasty Teacher   You'll ruin your skirt.

M6   I know, that's the point! Hated it. Could never figure it out. The only conclusion I came up with was that they made it a school rule just to get at me, just to irritate me.

M1   And of course I thought I was right because I was fourteen, and at fourteen I knew everything – well, according to my mum I did.

Mum   Oh, you think you know everything, don't you?

M1   Yes, Mum, I do.

M4   Unfortunately though, as the term progressed I realised I knew nothing.

MUSIC: 'We Can Work It Out.'

Little Girls Can't

Y1   For years they've dictated what I can and can't be, what I should and shouldn't do. And me, from four,

Y2   from three,

Y1   who knows, but I compromised, tried to please them, do what came naturally but not try to question their words, how could I at four,

Y2   at three?

Y1   And they told me:

Nasty Teacher   little girls can't, little girls mustn't. Mustn't climb trees, can't have a gun, can't be Napoleon Solo or Illya Kuryakin. Can't be Batman or Superman. Mustn't rough and tumble and fight, can't get covered in mud and grease and dirt. Little girls can't do what boys do, little girls mustn't be like little boys.

Y3   And they backed me into a corner. Didn't have the ability then at four,

Y2   at three,

Y3   to scream

Y1–4   liar,

Y3   was confused, didn't understand, wanted to climb trees, wanted to get dirty, wanted to rough and tumble and fight. Was a small thing but was important at four

Y2   at – (*Gets silenced.*)

Y4   So I compromised, pretended, in my head.

Y1–4   Be a boy

Y4   I said,

Y1–4   become a boy.

Y4   It was common, tomboy, hoyden, it's in the dictionary, it happens a lot to little girls, brainwashing. Brainwashing myself, subverting myself, turning myself into a boy

Nasty Teacher   because little girls can't and little girls don't,

Y1   but I could

Y1, Y2   and I did

Y1, Y2, Y3   and I wanted to.

Y4   So became a boy,

Y1   then at four,

Y2   at three even.

Y3   Felt confident then,

Y4   could do it then,

Y1   could run

Y2   and shout

Y3   and climb

Y4   and fight

Y1   and not be afraid to join in, not be afraid to test myself and explore the world.

Y3   And even then I saw it, even then at four,

Y2   at three;

Y3   fluffy little pink things standing on the sidelines watching, waiting, crying, clutching their dollies and being afraid.

Y4   And they were afraid because they couldn't practise,

Nasty Teacher   because little girls can't practise, little girls don't practise, little girls mustn't practise. Little girls can only stand on the sidelines and watch.

Y4   Practising only to grow older and stand on the sidelines and watch.

Beatles Fanatic

Y4   And then at seven, at eight, my world growing. Looking around me and I saw Beatles, Rolling Stones, pop groups, gods, idols, objects of worship like Jesus. And I see they are men, they are all men. I see men are worshipped, I see men are idolised, I see men are gods, and I see Sandy Shaw and Lulu. And I'm asked to choose a role model, a hero. And Sandy Shaw and Lulu, they don't speak, they can't speak, they can only sing and look pretty, look shyly at the camera and smile and wear dresses, pretty dresses and pretty smiles.

Y3   But the Beatles speak, they're allowed to speak, they're listened to. They're allowed a point of view, a sense of humour, they're allowed personalities. And I think back, I think back to Napoleon Solo and Illya Kuryakin

Y2   and Batman and Superman

Y1   and the Prisoner and the Saint

Y4   and Dr Who and James Bond

Y1   and Man in a Suitcase

Y2   and Randall and Hopkirk Deceased

Y3   and I'm beginning to learn, I realise I have been learning from four,

Y2   from three,

Y3   that the only thing I can do, the only thing I can aim for, the only thing that's accepted and applauded is manhood, is to be a man. And I'm not

Y2   but I practise, I'm still allowed to be a tomboy

Y1, Y3, Y4   at seven, at eight.

Y2   So the Beatles become my heroes, the Beatles become my role models because

Y1, Y3, Y4   at seven, at eight,

Y2   the Beatles are the most accepted and the most applauded and I've got to aim high, I've got to aim the highest, because I'm not really a man, I'm not really a boy, I'm only a tomboy, which is only second best, but at least it's higher than a fluffy pink little girl, at least it's higher than Sandy Shaw and Lulu.

Y1   And I become a Beatle fanatic,

Y4   a Beatle maniac.

Y3   I eat, sleep, think, dream Beatles,

Y2   I watch television about Beatles,

Y1   I read reports about Beatles and realise I'm not allowed to scream, I'm not allowed to faint, I'm not allowed to cry and I'm not allowed to wet myself because they laugh, it's laughed at, the girls, the fans, it's scorned, it's derided, the girls, the Beatle maniacs, but not the Beatles.

Y4   So I stop being a fan, I stop being a Beatle maniac and I become a Beatle, I become John. I have a Beatle haircut, and I wear shorts at playtime, I'm forbidden trousers but I'm allowed shorts at playtime and I see pictures of Beatles in shorts on bubble-gum cards, so I compromise, I'm happy, I'm a Beatle on a bubble-gum card.

Y2   And sometimes I'm Paul,

Y4   but mostly I'm John and I continue to brainwash and I continue to subvert because I don't want to be laughed at, I don't want to be derided, I don't want to stand on the sidelines humiliated and degraded and reduced to watching.

Y1   I want to join in.

Y3   I've got energy.

MUSIC: 'Yellow Submarine.'

Brownies and Cubs

Y2   When I was a kid I was in the Brownies.

Chorus Girls   (*sing*) We're the ever helpful gnomes

Helping others in their homes

We're the fairies bright and gay
Helping others every day.

We're the ever helpful pixies
Helping others in their fixes.

Y1–4   Here we are the sussed out elves

Helping no one but ourselves.

Y2   I left the Brownies.

Y1   I wanted to be in the Cubs,

Y3   the Cubs was good, the Cubs were exciting,

Y4   the Cubs were doing knots –

Chorus Boys   Wow, knots.

Y2   Later on I tried the Guides, but left in disgust, they were doing knots, it was so childish.

MUSIC: 'Yellow Submarine.'

Cookery Class

M1   And at eleven, at twelve, it's big school. I go to big school and learn needlework and cookery, and I wonder if John Lennon can sew, and deep down I know he can't, but then I realise that prisoners do, as a punishment in prison mailbags are sewn and that sounds interesting, that sounds heroic. So for the next five years I'm a misguided armed robber from a broken home, sewing mailbags once a week. And I continue to brainwash and I continue to subvert and once a week in cookery I'm stuck, because I can't seem to connect this activity, I can't find anything in it, I'm beginning to wonder what's the point, it's so boring, till the cookery teacher bounds in and says,

Cookery Teacher   How to make pastry to be proud of.

M1   And then it hits me, I realise I'm learning to cook for my future husband, that's it, that's all, there's nothing else, that's my life, learning to feed my future family.

M4   And I think this isn't me, this isn't John, it isn't an armed robber, so I make my stand, a silent protest, I forget my cookery basket. I can't carry a cookery basket.

M2   I leave it at home,

M3   leave it at the bus stop,

M5   leave it on the bus,

M6   throw it over a hedge,

M4   just get rid of it, and as a punishment instead I'm forced to wash pans, forced to wash pans with a scouring pad, and I think, good, another five years of imprisonment and punishment and pretending to be an old lag, thanks a lot Miss.

M1   And in big school I'm still forbidden trousers, I'm still forced to wear easy access clothing for the boys, but the problem isn't just knickers any more it's the whole body, it's growing and sprouting things.

Pilots and Doctors

M4   And in big school there is no playtime, there's only breaks and dinner-times and shorts are forbidden, so the question for the next five years is

M1–6   why is John Lennon wearing a skirt?

M1   And at eleven, at twelve, in big school there's something else, now there's subtlety and an insidious feeling that boys are getting a proper education and I'm being tolerated

M2   and boys are looking for careers

M3   and I'm waiting for my wedding day

M5   and boys are taken seriously

M6   and I'm a joke.

M4   And the brainwashing comes thick and fast now, the subversion is desperate because I realise I'm beginning to fade, I'm ceasing to exist.

M1   And the class is asked what they want to be and boys say,

B1–10   Airline Pilot,

M4   and girls say,

G1–6, F1–3   Air Hostess.

M1   And boys say,

B1–10   Doctor,

M4   and girls say,

G1–6, F1–3   Nurse.

M1   And boys say,

B1–10   Management Executive,

M4   and girls say,

G1–6, F1–3   Secretary.

M2   And I, John, and the other tomboys we just look, we just stare and say nothing because there's nothing we can say, we haven't even been included, because we've faded, we've ceased to exist.

M3   And I look around me and I see no more Napoleon Solo or Illya Kuryakin, no more Batman or Superman, no more Beatles. I see only firsts and seconds and lines being drawn and eyes being closed so I shut up about John Lennon.

M5   I shut up but secretly I brainwash and secretly I subvert and I don't know why anymore but it's habit, and it seems somehow to be a necessity, and it seems somehow to be survival,

M6   because I can't help thinking that really I don't want to be just a second-class girl.

Tights and Shoes

MUSIC: 'With a Little Help From My Friends.'

M4   My best friends, Paul, George and Ringo, the Fab Four, we went round in a gang, tomboys, until these (*tights*) walked into the classroom. On Paul's legs.

M1   I thought they looked silly,

M2   I thought they looked cold,

M1   I said to her,

M3   What are you doing for heaven's sake, that's the sort of thing my mum wears, and she's practically forty-six.

M5   And as if that wasn't bad enough then Ringo started wearing them – just because Paul did,

M2   And then even George

M4   the quiet one!

M1   And then when this happened to Paul

Chorus Boy   (*pulls up* **F1** *skirt*) 'whooo!'

M2   I was up, I was ready,

M6   ready to jump on the boy and Knicker Factor him.

M4   But what did Paul do? She went

F1   oh, for heaven's sake why don't you just grow up you stupid boy!

M1   Well, where's the fun in that? There is none.

M4   Something started happening to my friends –

M2   do you want a game of football?

F1–3   Nah.

M3   Want a game of wrestling?

F1–3   Nah.

M6   Well, do you wanna just slouch around then?

F1–3   Nah, I think I'll just sit like this thanks. (*Sits in a ladylike fashion.*)

M1   Toe ache. They must have got toe ache, because they started wearing these (*High-heeled shoes.*)

M2   Then they must have started thinking their legs looked really good, they must have thought their legs looked marvellous, because they started doing this (*Rolls up skirt to really short.*)

M1, M2   Now what can you do?

M4   Nothing.

M6   Well you could stand there, looking pretty and showing everybody your legs, I suppose.

M5   Gets a bit boring after a while though. So what's the point of that?

M6   And then I noticed something. The Knicker Factor. They've taken the Knicker Factor to extremes. They've made it so that they're almost showing their knickers all the time, but we never actually see their knickers again. Ever. Because for some reason the boys go nowhere near them, the boys avoid them like the plague, the boys are suddenly scared stiff of them.

M1–6   Wow!

M4   And my friends stand there saying,

F1–3   Go on, I dare you, go on. (*Dare to lift skirt.*)

M6   And they don't! Brilliant! But it's a bit drastic, isn't it? A bit restrictive. Still that's alright, I've got my skirt down to my knees and my socks up to my knees,

M4   but we're still best friends, still a gang, we're still getting on all right.

Mum Loves Pink

M3 However, I am not getting on all right with my mother. My mother is suggesting that I be

Mum a bit more glamorous.

M3 That it would be

Mum a good idea if we both went into town

M3 so that she

Mum could help you choose some clothes.

M3 I don't think so, Mum, I mean after all you are practically forty-six aren't you. She thinks

Mum it's not such a good idea for you to play football any more

M3 since I might

Mum get kicked in the stomach and drop your womb.

M3 She thinks my hair

Mum could do with a bit of body –

M3 which bit? An arm, a leg? – My face

Mum could do with a bit of colour

M3 and she thinks

Mum pink would suit you –

M3 but I don't like pink, Mum.

Mum But it suits you.

M3 But I don't like it.

Mum Well you're going to have to learn to like it because it suits you.

M3 She says I'd do better if I

Mum   pulled your shoulders back, sat properly and didn't slouch –

M3   do better at what? Sitting? I've done that since I was two and I haven't fallen over yet. And every time I go anywhere she says,

Mum   watch the buses,

Dad   don't talk to any strange men, don't let the boys get away with it, remember you're a nice girl from a nice home

Mum   and have you got a clean handkerchief?

M3   I'm only going to the pictures with me mates, Mum.

MUSIC: 'I Wanna Hold Your Hand.'

At the Pictures

All chorus enter and create cinema scene.

M4   At the pictures there were eight of us. Ringo was snogging very loudly with a boy while Paul and George were tutting and complaining about four lads who were throwing bits of paper round the audience and being obnoxious.

M5   The rest of us were throwing bits of paper round the audience and being obnoxious. It didn't occur to me though 'till I was half way home that girls just don't seem to have fun any more, I mean they giggle a lot, but they don't do anything.

MUSIC: Pearl and Dean.

Pathetic Actresses

M5   And at the pictures,

G1   I saw chicks in the flicks in the background like a Christmas tree listening to the male talk, never joining in.

G2   Or tarts in small parts, trying to steal the scene, looking sexy with a cigarette.

G3   Or dolly birds in mini skirts working as a secretary, filing her nails and looking for a brain.

G4   Or mumsy dumb housewives, happy little home-makers, washing the dirt 'till it's washing powder white.

G5   Or prancing, dancing, semi-naked nymphettes who you just know are there to titillate and then be attacked.

G6   And I wondered why that girl in the film was standing there screaming while her boyfriend battles with the intruder –

G1   screaming, you stupid cow, what's the point of that?

G2   Why don't you join in and help your boyfriend?

G3   Why don't you kick him, phone the police at least?

G4   Why don't you hit him with that dirty great vase that's right by your elbow?

G5   or you faint, you faint. He's chasing you, he's going to kill you, you're going to be murdered and you faint, you weak, pathetic girl,

G1   or you stumble, you stumble in those useless, impractical but highly fashionable sling-back, peep-toe high heels –

G6   oh god, women.

G2   What's the point of them,

G3   what earthly good do they do except get in the way, get under your feet,

G4   hold up the action with wet, boring romance, whining on about how she can't live without him

G5   when everybody knows he's only got fifteen minutes to save the world.

MUSIC: 'I Wanna Hold Your Hand.'

One of the Lads?

M2   So I hung around with the boys for a while,

B1   playing football

M2   and waiting for my womb to drop.

B2   We said 'fuck' every other word

B3   and smoked cigarettes pretending to be adults.

B4   Typical lads.

M2   And I was one of them, or so I thought 'till we walked past a park bench with three frozen girls on it.

G1–6   They giggled

B1–10   and we stopped. The boys nudged each other, looked shy and kicked the ground

G1–6   while the girls started preening themselves and trying to look aloof.

M2   I thought this was barmy. What are they doing? So I sat down next to them and started talking. Aren't you a bit cold in that strapless thing?

G1   Yes, I am a bit. I'm frozen actually.

M2   Well, why don't you put a cardigan on?

G2   Ooh, she couldn't, it would spoil the effect.

G3   Been playing football?

M2   Yeah.

G4   Yeah I know, we were watching you.

B1–10   The boys are still kicking the ground and being embarrassed,

M2   but not me, I think this is great, I think this is perfect because I feel just like John Lennon chatting to a Beatles fan

G5   who won't stop giggling,

M2   I'm in heaven – until one of the boys pipes up and shouts at the gigglers,

B7   Oi, she's a girl you know.

M2   Thank you, they do now. Well needless to say it was embarrassing, and I was

B5–10   ostracised by the boys from then on.

M2   Not my fault I'm better looking than they are.

Getting Ready

M4   So it's back to the girls' camp and things are moving apace.

F1   We're going to a dance on Saturday, do you wanna come?

M4   Yeah, all right, what time?

F2   Come to my house about two.

M4   What time's the dance?

F3   Eight.

M4   What are we going to do all afternoon?

M1   Stupid me, I turn up like this more or less with a couple of LPs under my arm thinking we're in for a fun afternoon and I end up sitting on the bed singing 'Help' while the other three prepare.

MUSIC: 'Help.'

Make Up

F1   Ooh, that's a lovely colour, can I borrow some?

F2   Don't nudge me, oh look I've smudged it now, I'm going to have to start all over again, and it's three o'clock already.

F3   We'll never be ready in time.

M4   Even George the quiet one.

F2 *blots lipstick with tissue paper.*

M1   Finally I say,

M4   why are you doing this?

F1   You've got to!

F2   Wanna borrow some?

M4   No thanks.

F3   Wanna borrow a dress?

M4   No thanks.

F1   Wanna borrow a skirt?

M4   No thanks.

F2   Touch of lipstick?

M4   No.

F3   Bit of colour for your cheeks?

M4   You sound like my mother.

F1, F2, F3   All right, but you'll be sorry.

M4   I won't.

M1   I was.

MUSIC: Loud party music (1960s cheesy).

At the Dance

All cast and chorus enter.

M6   At the dance we were laughing and dancing and giggling and talking, guzzling Coca Cola, smoking cigarettes,

M5   pretending to be adults

Males   and then the boys arrived.

M5   Phoom,

Females   all the girls disappear into the toilets,

M6   I didn't know, hadn't been told the rules.

M5   So I sat there and watched the boys prepare.

Males   Guzzling Coca Cola – ta – and smoking cigarettes pretending to be adults – ta.

M6   Then the toilet door flies open

Females   and out all the girls parade.

Mum   A hundred and one different varieties of cheap perfume getting to their seats before them.

M5   Positions are taken

Females   girls on one side of the room

Males   boys on the other,

M5   and then it starts.

M6   The dance hall turns into a shooting gallery at the fairground,

Dad   the boys have the rifles

Mum   and the girls are the targets, the sitting ducks.

Males   Some of the boys take aim and shoot off.

B2   Would you like to dance?

G1   Oh all right. I've been picked. Isn't he lovely, isn't he gorgeous? You're all right I suppose . . . Fancy a snog?

M6   Some of the boys miss badly.

B1   Would you like to dance?

G2   Shove off, spotty!

M5   Then he can't get back.

B1   I can't get back.

M6   Sweat pours off him,

B1   sweat's pouring off me.

M5   His eyes bulge.

B1   Me eyes are bulging.

M6   Nobody's taking the blindest bit of notice of him,

B1   everybody's looking at me, and it's three miles!

M5   Finally a friend rescues him,

B1   ugly cow, I only asked her cus I felt sorry for her.

M6   And so it goes, on and on, all night, till there's only one left.

M5   Me.

Lonely

M5   So after the forty-second round of playing sitting ducks at a shooting gallery and never once getting shot, I decided I wasn't happy, I wasn't winning,

M6   I'm a little bit lonely

M5   and I might be wrong.

Return of the Skirt

M2   There's something wrong with me. There's something seriously wrong with me. Everywhere I go girls my age are growing up, wanting to grow up, going shopping, trying on clothes and enjoying it. Discussing make up, boyfriends, and not getting bored. Talking about engagements, weddings, even discussing babies and looking forward to it. And me, there's something wrong with me because I can't even feel comfortable in dresses, skirts, anything that shows my legs . . . Anything that makes me feel female – I don't know why.

M3   And my mum thinks I'm stupid because I've worn a skirt

Mum, Dad   every school-day since you were five,

M2   and I say

M3   I know, but it was different then, I had to. I want to grow up and make my own decisions, choose my own clothes, be my own person.

M2   And my mum says,

Mum   It's about time you grew up because you won't get a job in jeans, not one that's interesting anyway.

M2   And I say,

M3   I don't care, I'd rather be a road sweeper than have to wear a dress!

M2   And my mum says,

Mum   Well why for heaven's sake, what's the matter with you?

M3   And I shut up and just give her a look, because I don't know why, I just feel like a freak.

M2   And my dad says,

Dad   Well anyway you can't be a road sweeper, that's a man's job.

M2   And I go to interviews and interviews and interviews and finally slam out and go and buy a skirt because I'm beginning to hate this world

M3   and I'm beginning to think I'm going mad.

Patronising Parents

M2   I shouldn't have to do this, I don't want to do this, I'm getting a reputation for being ugly. I can't hang around with the boys any more in case somebody thinks I'm an ugly girlfriend and I can't hang around with the girls any more in case somebody thinks I'm a boyfriend.

M3   I tried sitting at home but all I get is sympathetic looks from my parents and a pep talk from my mum.

Mum   No, you're not ugly, you've got a lovely face, you have, it's just like mine. But you've got to do something with it. I mean look at your hair – fluff it up a bit.

M3   I don't want it fluffed up, Mum.

Mum   Put a bit of colour on your cheeks, you could look like Audrey Hepburn.

M3   I don't want to look like Audrey Hepburn!

Mum   Well, you've got to glamourise yourself, I did at your age and I could have had any man I chose.

M3   Well why did you choose Dad then?

On the Bus

M4   One day I was sitting on the bus going to school

Girl on Bus   and a fluffy pink little girl was sitting opposite

Mum on Bus   with her mummy

Girl on Bus   on the side seats.

M4   And she looked at me then she said in a really loud voice

Mum on Bus   for the whole bus to hear,

M4   she said,

Girl on Bus   Mummy, why is that boy wearing a skirt?

M4   And I looked at her,

Girl on Bus   fluffy pink little buck-toothed cry-baby

M4   and I said in an equally loud voice

Mum on Bus   for the whole bus to hear,

M4   My dear girl I am not a boy

M1–6   I am John Lennon!

M4   That's told her I thought,

Mum on Bus   and the rest of the world come to that.

MUSIC: When I Saw Her Standing There.

Boyfriends

B1   My first boyfriend stood me up outside the cinema.

M1   I say boyfriend although he wasn't technically, since we never actually got together,

B1   but when it's your first you've got to say something.

B2   My second boyfriend met me outside the cinema, took me in, sat me down and then started grappling with my tits and my mouth

M1   – I'm not sure if it was for his benefit or mine, but I wasn't very keen. Missed half film as well, mostly going

M1–6   Don't. Milk. Me!

B3   My third boyfriend was great

M1   on his own,

B3   but ninety per cent of the time insisted on us going everywhere with his mates so that he could talk to them

M1   and parade me like a trophy.

B4   My fourth boyfriend talked to me all the time,

M1   I never once got a word in edgeways.

B4   He said he loved girls because they were such good listeners.

M1   He then said,

B4   How about it?

M1   My fifth boyfriend was really nice

M3   so I said how about it?

B6   My sixth boyfriend spent a useful couple of hours telling me the trouble with women was their hormones, their frigidity and their desperate ambition to get married.

M1   We weren't suited, only lasted a couple of hours.

B7   My seventh boyfriend was a proper gentleman, full of respect for females, did everything for me –

M1   including thinking, which I thought was very nice of him, since I'd never have been able to do it on my own.

B8   My eighth boyfriend called me a feminist lesbian every time I disagreed with his opinions and

B9   my ninth boyfriend called me a brainless chick every time I didn't offer one.

B10   My tenth boyfriend was a real revolutionary, even looked like Che Guevara, believed totally in women's liberation but only after the working class revolution,

O4   I presume that's the working class male revolution?

B10   Don't nit pick.

O4   I won't,

M1   I can't be bothered.

That's Not Me

M1–6   In between times I went dancing with the girls.

MUSIC: 1970s Hippie.

'Johns' *start to dance on their own, perfectly happily, then* **Girls** *and* **Mum** *enter and cover them in pink accessories, spoiling their fun.*

O1   That's not me. I'm not like that. I'm only doing this so that I've got some friends, so that they don't think I'm a freak.

O2   So that I don't think I'm a freak,

O1   but I am one,

O3   I must be because I just feel worse, I feel stupid, I feel really silly dressed like this.

O4   I only did it because I was fed up being called ugly, but then I never particularly wanted to be pretty in the first place, and I certainly don't feel pretty dressed like this, and I only did it because I was lonely, but I've never felt lonelier than in this stupid dress and this stupid make up . . . So get it off me, take it off me.

O1   And if you want to call me a freak you can call me a freak because I don't care, can't be any worse, can't be any worse than that stuff,

O2   having to shut up and sit there and smile and try to look pretty for the boys, having to play sitting ducks, hoping to get lucky or something stupid like that.

O3   I'm sick of it, never wanted to be a girl in the first place, don't know how to be one anyway so why should I bother trying, it's stupid.

O4   I'm not going to sit there, smiling and pretending I'm not as clever as you just because I'm supposed to want a boyfriend –

O1   I don't want a boyfriend.

O2   Well, not if he's just going round with a dress and a bit of make up on his arm I don't.

O3   It's stupid, it's pointless,

O4   and it's not me.

This Is Me!

O1   And I interrupted

O2   and I argued

O3   and I questioned

O4   and I disagreed

O1, O2   and I refused to pretend,

O3, O4   refused to conform.

O1   And I refused to insult anybody by wearing this stuff, because who's he going out with? That's not me – that's just a dress, he's going out with a dress, and I refused to insult myself by wearing this stuff, because I thoroughly believed it was this stuff's fault.

O2   Wearing this stuff is dangerous, wearing this stuff makes you wilt, makes it impossible to move, impossible to talk, impossible to think, impossible to breathe – this stuff just forces you to smile and panic at the same time.

O3   This is me. Dressing how I want to dress and thinking what I want to think. And I did it and it was fun. I still had friends, I was still popular, still went out, went dancing, and if there was a boy I danced with a boy, and if there was a girl I danced with a girl. If there was nobody I danced by myself . . .

O4   I didn't care. I flung myself and I threw myself and my nails broke, my hair was all over the place, my clothes were a mess, my face was a mess and I didn't care. I just had so much energy. And my legs grew hair, my armpits grew hair, my eyebrows grew bushy – I thought I was turning into a werewolf . . .

MUSIC: 'Get Back.'

Women's Lib

O1   Women's lib,

O2   women's liberation,

O3, O4   the Women's Liberation Movement.

Y1–4   Oh wow, that's like the French Resistance,

M1–6   like freedom fighters,

O1–4   that's something heroic.

Y1–4   That's what I want,

M1–6   that's what I could do,

O1   fighting for freedom, liberation, I could be a real hero.

O2   Women's lib . . .

O3   There'd be espionage and sabotage,

O4   intrigue, excitement, danger,

Y1–4   running, lots of running,

M1–6   and physical exertion, physical sweat.

O1   I saw them on the telly, burning their bras,

O2   they were on the news, they're important, they were being interviewed.

O3   I don't know what they said but they don't wear dresses or skirts or make up or tights either, they're probably just like me, they probably hate being female too.

O4   But when we've all got together and fought a few battles, shown the world that we're not just silly little acquiescent china dolls, then we can start to like ourselves, start to realise that it's okay to be female,

Y1–4   it's good to be female,

M1–6   that we can be girls and gutsy heroes at the same time.

O1   And I can do it then, I can stop brainwashing, stop subverting.

O2   I can be female and be proud, stop feeling ashamed, stop hiding, covering up, stop feeling second class, stop being a stupid boy.

O3   I can start to like myself, start to love myself, be myself.

O4   Women's lib, it'll be great, it'll be like the Fab Four would have been if they hadn't started wearing those stupid tights.

M1   We'll get motorbikes.

M2   We'll ride around in packs on motorbikes like Hell's Angels

M3   looking scruffy but confident and in control,

M4   and we'll liberate women,

M5   we'll liberate girls.

M6   . . . We'll liberate anyone, we don't mind, you want liberating, send for us.

Y1   We'll start off with schools first,

Y2   we'll go round to the board of governors

Y3   and force them to change the rules about skirts

Y4   unless they can come up with a reasonable explanation as to why.

M1   Force them to put self defence on the curriculum

M2   – ju-jitzu for girls only, instead of needlework,

M3   unless it's poison dart needlework of course,

M4   so that they can learn to defend themselves, fight back,

M5   and not have to worry about who's stronger or weaker or bigger or smaller,

M6   so they can learn to stand up for themselves and be confident.

O1   We'll set up refuges for battered women, battered children, battered anybodies, they tell us who and we go round and batter the batterer.

O2   If he complains, says it's not fair because it's four against one, we'll say,

O1–4   We don't care, we're no longer going to be the fairer sex pal!

O2   Then we'll cheerfully duff him up, teach him a lesson.

O3   And on our days off we'll go round court rooms and laugh and snigger at the judge in his stupid wig and stupid gown and we'll say,

O1–4   Oi, darling, where'd you get your frock? You're asking for it wearing that frock aren't you judgey wudgey baby?

O4   And we'll go round publishing houses where they make girls' comics and women's magazines and we'll threaten to blow up the building unless they print stories and articles showing exciting and adventurous females,

M1–3   women being courageous,

Y1, Y2   women being brave,

Y3, Y4   saving the world

M4–6   and getting their man

O4   so people can say,

O1–3   Oh yeah, I want to be a women's libber, that's more interesting than slimming stories and beauty tips!

Y1, Y2   But most of all it'll be fun,

Y3, Y4   women's liberation is going to be such fun,

M1, M2   we'll ride around together,

M3, M4   laughing and giggling

M5, M6   and showing the world how great it is to be female,

O1   how bloody marvellous it is to be female

O2   when you're the sort of female you want to be and

O3   not what you're supposed to be

O4   or expected to be.

Women's Meeting

All females enter.

O4   And then I went to a meeting. A women only group. And I said, 'Who's in charge?' and they said,

Females   We all are.

O4   And they talked about sisterhood and patriarchy and politics – or more to the point, how they hated men. And I said, 'Doesn't anybody hate women? Doesn't anybody hate being a woman? Doesn't anybody hate being thought of as kind and gentle and understanding and supportive and patient and democratic and nurturing and reasonable and non-aggressive and helpful and self-sacrificing and fair-minded and co-operative? Doesn't anybody hate being thought of as nice? Like a biscuit? Doesn't anybody want to be a hero? Doesn't anybody just love what men do and want to do it too? Isn't there anybody here who's insanely jealous that they weren't born a boy? That they weren't born with the opportunity to do anything they wanted to do without having to apologise or justify or explain or feel guilty or awkward or feel like a freak or be ridiculed or persecuted or ostracized or wait 'till it's fashionable?' And they said,

Females   No.

O4   And I said, 'What's wrong with me then? Why am I such a freak? Why can't I just be a woman. What are you then? What is a woman?' And they said,

Females   Oppressed.

O4   Fine. Be that then.

MUSIC: 'Let It Be.'

World of Work

O3   And my Careers Officer asked me what I wanted to be –

O2   I said,

O3   John Lennon.

O2   She said,

Careers Officer   Yes, but how about Nurse?

O2   I said,

O3   Is there a skirt involved?

O2   She said,

Careers Officer   Yes.

O2   I said,

O3   No.

O2   She said,

Careers Officer   How about Secretary?

O2   I said,

O3   Skirt?

O2   She said,

Careers Officer   Yes.

O2   I said,

O3   No. She thought I was stupid, but I thought she was because she was wearing a skirt and I wasn't.

First Job

O2   My first job was with a very classy firm. Or so the personnel lady told me.

Personnel Officer   Oh yes, we've got branches in America you know, so we expect all our employees to dress accordingly.

O1   I thought it was a bit like school, except that all the girls could wear anything they wanted to wear so long as their legs were on show, and all the boys could wear anything they wanted to wear so long as it was a shirt and tie and jacket and long ones down to here (*Ankles.*) and nice lace-up shiny shoes.

O2   And all the boys flirted with all the girls, and all the men flirted with all the girls, and all the girls did all day was talk about the boys and the men flirting with them, good or bad.

O1   I worked with two other girls and I knew I wasn't going to fit in the first time they took me to the canteen at lunch time. They ordered boeuf bourgignon and I didn't know what it was so had a cheese sandwich and sat for an hour feeling intimidated and working class while they scoured the room hoping to chat to

Mr Banks   Mr Banks from Accounts because he was really good looking and wouldn't you just love to melt into his arms?

O2   Well no I wouldn't actually,

O1   I was too busy trying not to melt into the woodwork every time he was around.

O2   He did nothing but shout all the time.

O1   He had a very novel way of working, he'd scrawl a lot of words onto one piece of paper, give it to me and I'd type the same words onto another piece of paper – talk about trees. If I couldn't work out what it said I'd go into his office and he'd say,

Mr Banks   Why can't you work out what it says, do I have to be interrupted every five minutes, what are we paying you for?

O2   And then I wouldn't bother going into his office, and then he'd come out and say,

Mr Banks   What is this? This is rubbish, I never wrote this, look that's suspend the account, not suspect the account, you stupid girl!

O1   And the other girls would laugh and pull faces behind my back because they were friends and I wasn't, and I knew it was because of this skirt – I felt embarrassed and intimidated and on show, I felt like a sexual diversion for the men,

B10   all trying to get their leg over at lunch time or something,

B9   coming up close and putting their arms around me,

B8   calling me darling or love and stuff

O2   with their BO and bad breath and sheer ugliness.

O1   And they thought I was gormless and thick, and I thought I'm becoming gormless and thick and I thought I've got to do something about it otherwise this skirt is going to make me burst into tears.

O2   And that's not the sort of thing I like to do in public, and especially not in front of those girls.

In The Army

O3   Being as this was

Personnel Officer   a classy firm with branches in America

O3   I went out and bought some culottes

O1   because they're French and France is just as classy as America,

O2   if not more so in my opinion.

O3   And I wore them to work and nobody said anything, nobody told me to go home and change, and I thought

O1–O4   good.

O2   I thought I'm not going to play their game anymore, I'm not going to be some tarty typist or some stupid secretary bird, I'll play my own game,

O1–O4   and I did,

O3   because I looked at myself and I thought I looked like a private, in the army, in Burma. Yes that's what I'll be and then they won't chat me up,

O1–O4   but they did.

O3   So I got some socks.

O1–4   That's the game.

O3   I'm a private in the army in Burma

Mr Banks   and the boss is a Sergeant Major, so of course he shouts, he's supposed to shout, it's his job, it's nothing personal.

O1   And the more he shouts the better soldier I become,

O2   I might even make Corporal

O4   and then they won't chat me up,

O1–O4   but they did.

O3   So I got some boots. Some big private-in-the-army-in-Burma boots and I thought they won't chat me up now,

O1–O4   but they did, they just thought I was wacky, but I didn't care because I marched around all day looking efficient

O1   – I wasn't actually efficient, I just looked efficient

O4   and that's what counts in offices.

Mr Banks   And any time the boss shouted I'd just say,

O1–O4   Yes sir!

O3   – And carry on marching.

B8, B9, B10   And any time they'd try to chat me up

O3   I'd just say,

O1–O4   That contravenes regulations

O3   – and carry on marching.

O1   I loved it because it was my game

Mr Banks   and the boss was playing my game, and he was playing it wonderfully, shouting away like Sergeant Majors are supposed to, great,

O2 couldn't wait to get to work in the morning so that I could hear him shout and I could say,

O1–O4 Yes sir.

O3 Felt so confident, so courageous.

O4 Ruined it though, got carried away, because he called me into his office one day and I marched in and said,

O1–O4 Yes, Sergeant Major, sir! (*Salutes.*)

O3 Got court-martialled.

O1 Oh well, Civvy Street then.

O2 Civvy Street and demob trousers.

O4 Aren't they awful, aren't they horrible?

O3 Great, they won't chat me up in these and if there's one thing I've learnt it's that I'm never going to wear a uniform again.

Woman or Boy?

MUSIC: 'Strawberry Fields Forever.'

O4 Got a job in an arts centre, in the café cooking carrot cake. (I started that trend, only did it as a joke, didn't expect anybody to eat it!) Only applied for the job because everybody was wearing jeans, never once saw a leg the whole time I was there, thought I've got to fit in here, it's got to be here, there's nowhere else. Course, it was very middle class, very right on,

O1 crawling with feminists

O2 having meetings,

O3 because everybody was in charge,

O4 can I move?

O1, O2, O3   – Can we discuss it?

O4   And while I was there I saw endless films, plays, cabarets, bands, poets, meetings, discussions, conversations, workshops, seminars, books, pamphlets, posters about

O1   women and poverty,

O2   women and misogyny,

O3   women and violence,

M1   women and sexuality,

M2   women and fear,

M3   women and crime,

M4   women in the workplace,

M5   women in the home,

M6   women with children,

O1   women without children,

O2   women with men,

O3   women with women,

Y1   women in isolation,

Y2   women in society,

Y3   women being confused,

Y4   women being used,

O1   women being abused,

O2   women being refused,

O3   women being repressed,

M1   women being suppressed,

M2   women being oppressed,

M3   women being depressed,

M4   women wanting equality,

M5   women wanting justice,

M6   women wanting freedom,

Y1–4   women wanting peace.

O4   And I got chatted up

O1   by a lesbian –

O4   no, I'm a boy. Got invited to women only meetings

O2, O3   by feminists –

O4   no, I'm a boy. Got coerced into a discussion about sexual politics and women's problems

B10   by a right on liberal man –

O4   I'm a boy. Got chatted up

B9   by a not so right on liberal man –

O4   I'm a boy. I'm a boy. I had energy. I'm a boy and I get annoyed at people who assume otherwise, I get annoyed at people who think it's a problem and want to put me straight, I get annoyed at people who think I'm some kind of traitor to some kind of Cause. I get annoyed at people who want to show me positive images of women, thinking all I need to do is read a book about goddesses and I'll be cured. I get annoyed at people who think it's lack of confidence, lack of beauty, lack of a boyfriend or lack of marbles, and I get raging at people who think it's man-hating because that's less logical than me saying I'm a boy in the first place. I'm a boy. I am. I ignore all this (*Below the neck.*) stuff –

O1   It's too fat

O2   it's too thin

O3   it's too tall

B10   it's too short

B9   too big

O1   too small

O2   not the right shape

O3   not the right size

B10   not the right colour

B9   not the right look,

O4   it's a woman's body, it's pathetic, I hate it,

O1   I want to hit it

O2   want to beat it up

O3   want to cover it in bruises

B10   want to mash it

B9   want to rip it up

O1   want to disfigure it

O2   want to destroy it

O3   want to kill it

B10   it's weak

B9   second rate

O1   second class

O2   second best

O3   it's passive

B10   it's apologetic

B9   it's guilt ridden

O1   it gets blamed for everything

O2   has to fight for everything

O3   fight itself

B10   fight other people

B9   fight every day

O4   and never win, never be a hero, so what's the point, keep it covered up and ignore it. Pretend it doesn't exist, stop fighting and have some fun.

MUSIC: 'Twist and Shout.'

Finally

Flexible line allocations – to be used to bring full cast and chorus onstage for the Curtain Call. Lines delivered either as specific characters or as the individuals themselves to bring it right up to date.

I took a crash course in out and out manhood. And I found the key. Society wanted me to be, and saw me as nothing more, nothing else, nothing other than breeding equipment, a womb, a womb-man.

Since four, since three, since birth even, they wanted me to be the future. No career, no hobbies, no brain, no mind, no thoughts other than the bearer of mankind, the carrier of creation.

Females from birth being trained to be pretty, to be attractive, to look in the mirror and say, 'That's all you've got' since two, since two years old, being put in silly little dresses.

Females from birth being trained to be passive, to be sedate, to smile and avoid danger and protect their wombs, avoid the danger of dropping their wombs. Get off the cricket pitch and go into the pavilion and make sandwiches, it's safer.

Females from birth being trained to rely on men to protect them.

Females from birth being told, 'Do whatever you want girls, but whatever you do don't lose your femininity' because femininity's just another word for future.

And then what? After that what?

Nothing.

Nothing more than what every female's been trained for: sacrifice, drudgery, being taken for granted, being tired, being worn out, putting my life on hold, putting my children first.

I looked around me and I saw women being told to be attractive, being told to be mothers and career women and home-makers and shoppers and lovers and wives.

Women being told to have it all, and do it all.

Being told to get to the top, and stay at the bottom.

Be the boss, and clean the house.

Women being told it's your decade, and your workload.

Being told there's jobs for women, because you're cheap.

Being told you can do everything and being told to prove everything.

Being told it's your world, and being told to turn it.

Being told you're in control now, you can do anything you want, but stay attractive and guilty and thin and smile and watch the men.

Because men are important, because men are the heroes and women can't be heroes.

They can't be heroes.

And I thought, 'No, I'm not going to play their games, I'd rather just drop my womb and be a boy, it's much more fun'.

MUSIC: The most contemporary, popular, anthemic, uplifting song as everybody leaves the stage.

Arsehammers

Adapted by Liz Light

This version of *Arsehammers* was first produced by **Stage2** at the Crescent Theatre, Birmingham, on 12 January 2011 with the following cast and creatives:

1	Laura Dowsett
2	Anna Gilmore
3	Peter Collier
4	Mark James
5	Kesia Schofield
6	Mia-Rose Yates
7	Gabriel Hudson
8	Meg Luesley
9	Sasha Butler
10	Rosie Nisbet
11	Roni Mevorach
12	Tom Baker
13	George Hannigan
14	Priya Edwards
15	Alice Bettis Marsh
16	Matt Childs
Grandad (*voice on tape*)	Peter Booth

Crew

Director Liz Light
Assistant Director/Line Allocations Ryan Fox
Production Manager/Lighting Designer Chris Cuthbert
Lighting Operator Tom Booth
Sound Operator Kara Spriggs
Backstage Manager Alex Pugh
Head Chaperone Lucy Bailey-Wright

Preset: Snakes and Ladders
Playing area 5m × 5m, marked out in 16 brightly coloured squares.

Cast using it as a board to play a game of Snakes and Ladders with themselves as counters and cut out giant snakes and ladders.

Performed in thrust with audience on three sides – on the fourth side, all cast have a toy placed in rows.

Number 1's toy is a large dice, which is being used in the game.

Lots of laughing, teasing and noisy playing. Everyone oblivious to audience entering.

Music
Music throughout is excerpts from a selection of the most recognisable wartime songs.

All cast play simple games e.g. marching, spinning, hop-scotch, etc. to intersperse the acting.

Costume
All cast in a mixture of bright, block colours – the same as the ones used in the squares on the set (three or four different colours each).

All children are young i.e. playing age 10/11 (Junior School, not Secondary). Items of clothing show differences in character/parts to convey that anyone can experience dementia in the family.

Characters

1
2
3
4
5
6
7
8
9
10
11
12
13
14
15
16
Grandad (*voice on tape*)

Scene 1: Family Album

1   Grandad has been living with Mum and Dad and Claudia and me for years.

Music 1

Everyone takes their toy, claims a square and acts out independent scenarios in their own world.

Scene 2: Angels + Claudia

2   Sometimes it seems like forever

15   but I can remember him coming.

13   I was a lot younger then

10   and remember that I couldn't make up my mind whether to be happy or sad.

12   I was sad when Mum told me that Grandma had gone to live with the angels

9   but I was also happy that Grandad was coming to live with us.

5   I had pestered Mum for ages

4   about Grandma changing her mind about the angels

14   and coming with Grandad to live with us instead.

3   I had, at the time,

11   thought Mum would be pleased

6   that I liked Grandma so much

7   and couldn't understand why she got so upset when I asked.

1   In the end I just wrote to the angels

16   thanking them for having Grandma

8   and asking that they take good care of her.

---

16   Now that I'm older, of course,

4   I feel really stupid about believing all that rubbish about angels,

12   there's no such thing as angels,

3   Grandma is dead, buried and living alone.

7   But I'm older and wiser now and know that if I don't quite understand something

13   it's always best to pretend I do and then get Claudia to ask the questions.

Music 2

Boys spoil girls' games (like skipping and elastics).

Scene 3: Beans on Toast (and Doom!)

14   And Grandad is living in our house. Well, so far.

9   Because I've overheard Mum and Dad talking about being unable to cope

2   and putting Grandad in a home.

1   This worries me.

14, 9, 2, 1   Beans on toast.

1 + 2   It's always beans on toast when Grandad goes missing.

Boys   I don't mind too much,

Girls   it's just that Mum always clatters the spoon noisily on the plate when she's serving out the beans

2   and she Talks!

+9   Like!

+14   This!

+1   About!

+Girls   Every!

+Boys   Thing!

9 + 14   If she bothers to talk at all.

1 + 2   It's at times like this that I'm glad Claudia's here.

7 + 12   I don't like Claudia, of course,

16 + 4   she's my little sister,

3 + 13   but at least I can pick a fight with her

Boys   and get Mum really shouting about something instead of

2   Talking!

+9   Like!

+14   This!

+1   All!

+Girls   The!

+Boys   Time!

Boys   And if Claudia and I get Mum shouting now,

Girls   she doesn't shout so much at Dad when he comes home.

10   I like Grandad, I'm glad Grandad lives with us.

8   But Mum and Dad have decided

5   that Grandad has to go into a home.

6   Grandad seems to be permanently missing.

15   And he's started shouting,

11   which Mum thinks 'could get out of hand'.

Boys   Claudia and I have been eating beans on toast for weeks on end,

1, 2, 14, 9   and Mum and Dad have been arguing for weeks on end,

14 + 9   so when Dad stays home from work

+2   and spends all day on the phone,

+1   I know Grandad is doomed.

Music 3

Individual and small group games (e.g. conkers, catch, etc), concentrating very hard and becoming anxious and irritable.

Scene 4: Arsehammers is Magic

13   Having Arsehammers is magic.

15   Sometimes you don't have them

13   and then all of a sudden,

All   bang,

13   you have them again.

12   This is how it is with Grandad.

16   Sometimes Grandad will go out of the house to visit his friends to talk about wars,

4   or queue at the post office to talk about queuing during wars

7   and, after a certain time,

3   he will come back again.

---

13   Unless the Arsehammers strike.

12   Then Grandad will go out of the house and disappear for hours,

16   ending up in the strangest of places and always miles away from his friends or the Post Office.

4   I often hear Mum on the phone or on the doorstep with the police demanding to be told exactly how Grandad managed to get himself locked in the cold meat storage facility of the supermarket or into the staff canteen of the foreign mail section of the postal sorting office.

7   Mum doesn't know. The police don't know either.

15   But I do,

3   Grandad has developed a special kind of bottom. Hammer shaped. And when he wiggles it in a certain direction he is magically transported to weird and wonderful places.

15   A bit like having special Star Trek powers, but without the Enterprise.

13   Grandad could be waiting for a bus one minute and the next –

All   Kaboom!

12   – he is watching traffic go by on the motorway.

16   This is what makes Grandad special

4   and a bit of a hero.

7   Because me and my friends have tried having Arsehammers

3   and it is impossible.

13   At a given signal

Girls   'Arsehammers!'

12   we close our eyes,

All   stick our bottoms out,

16   lurch them to the left,

4   lurch them to the right,

7   lurch them to the left again,

3   give a little wiggle,

13   bend our knees, squat as hard as possible and spring up as high as we can.

Boys   When we open our eyes, we should be transported to weird and wonderful places.

15   But we're not.

Girls   We're still in exactly the same spot.

13   Except once, when Robert transported himself further down the road.

15   Which proves we are on the right track

Girls   but need practice.

Music 4

Everybody practises the wiggle and does other general crazy acrobatics.

Scene 5: Staring into Space

All except **1** *and* **11** *make a giant, empty armchair.*

1   Sometimes Grandad will be sitting in an armchair staring into space.

11   Mum will say,

All   'Grandad's not with us today.'

(*not* **1** *or* **11**)

1   And I'll look at him,

11   sometimes with binoculars,

1   wondering where he is, exactly,

11   and how he got there.

1   When Grandad is here I often ask if, next time he goes, he'll take me with him.

11   But Grandad just looks at me strangely and changes the subject.

1 + 11   I find it very frustrating,

1   and sometimes get cross with Grandad and warn him that he'll end up in a home.

11   Grandad simply says,

Grandad   'Yes.'

(*voice on tape*)

Scene 6: How He Used to Be

8 + 5   When Grandad doesn't have Arsehammers, he is just plain Grandad, and plays games with Claudia and me,

8   or tells us stories about when he was a hero in the war.

8 + 5   I like him then as well.

5   There was a time when Grandad babysat but he doesn't any more because Mum 'doesn't trust him'.

8 + 5   This is a shame

8   because Grandad let us mess about before bed much more than Mum or Dad do

5   and he never minded the bath water splashing everywhere when we played Dive-Bombing Ducks.

Music 5

British Bulldogs (or Dive-Bombing Ducks).

Scene 7: Can I 'Play' Too?

13   Arsehammers is a game to my friends

11   but to me it is serious.

13   I don't want Grandad to go into a home.

11   I thought that if I could learn to be transported like Grandad maybe Grandad and I could go places together.

13   Then Mum and Dad wouldn't worry about Grandad being out all hours on his own.

11   I often watch Grandad, looking for clues.

13   I like Grandad,

11   Grandad's fun,

13   Grandad's a hero to me and my friends,

11   and Grandad's already living in a home,

11 + 13   our home.

Scene 8: Journey to the Home (+ The Army)

10   I sit with Grandad

6   and Claudia

10   in the back of the car, trying to make up my mind whether to be happy or sad as we drive out to put Grandad into the home. I'm happy because it is a day off school and Mum has made sandwiches for the journey, which means it will be a bit of an adventure going miles out of town.

6   But I'm also sad that Grandad is leaving.

10   Mum and Dad have said lots of times that we can visit him at the weekends, but it isn't the same. And even though Grandad and I haven't run around the house playing Germans and British for ages,

6   I was still hoping that someday we might.

Music 6

Marching in formations like soldiers.

Scene 9: Arrival at the Home

10   By the time we get to the home I have decided it is definitely a sad day.

9   Mum has made egg sandwiches, which I hate. And cheese sandwiches, which I hate even more than egg, and Claudia has been sick down her dress.

2   However, I feel a lot happier when we go inside Grandad's new home.

---

9   A lady with squeaky shoes shows us round the big house.

2   Lots of other Grandmas and Grandads live there.

9   And Grandad's room is a lot bigger than his old one

2   and it has a television and a button he can press if he wants 'Assistance'.

9   The lady smiles a lot and seems nice, so I ask her if all the other Grandmas and Grandads have Arsehammers.

2   She says, 'Yes, this is a special home with lots of experts who try to make things better for your Grandad and all the others like him.'

Scene 10: Experts and Happiness!

5, 8, 14, 15   I am over the moon.

8   It suddenly all makes sense to me,

5   Grandad isn't being put in a home.

14 + 15   Grandad is going to help save the world!

5, 8, 14, 15   Grandad is even more of a hero than he was before.

14 + 15   Experts.

8   Experts are going to train Grandad

5   and all the other people with Arsehammers

14   to transport themselves to proper places,

15   planned places,

8   where they can suddenly turn up and overthrow dastardly villains

5   and listen in to secret spy conversations,

14 + 15   and generally go where no man has gone before,

8   and suddenly appear and say,

All   'Boo'

5   and frighten the life out of the most hardened of criminals.

15   I laugh,

14   I am happy,

5, 8, 14, 15   I think Grandad will be happy here too.

Music 7

Happy spinning 'games' – crossed and linked arms, etc.

Scene 11: Mum is Upset

10   Mum is upset, though.

6   In the car going home she cries.

6 + 10   Claudia and I pretend not to notice

6   but she cries a lot.

10   When she stops crying and is just snuffling

6   Claudia asks her why Grandad isn't coming home with us.

6 + 10   Mum is quiet for a minute or two

2   before she turns round to explain to Claudia

9   that Grandad has a disease of the brain, called Alzheimers

6   which makes him very poorly and confused,

9   so that he forgets where he is,

2   where he is going,

2 + 9   who he is

6 + 10   and who Mum and Dad and me and Claudia are,

2, 9, 10   and that he has to stay in that special home because he will get worse and worse.

6   And then Mum starts crying again.

Scene 12: I Sulk – I Was Wrong

All   I sulk the rest of the way home.

> *Pull sulky face and make sulky noise.*

I sulk during tea.

> *Pull sulky face and make sulky noise.*

I sulk 'till bedtime.

> *Pull sulky face and make sulky noise.*

And then, when I go to bed, I sulk in bed as well.

11   *Pull sulky face and make sulky noise.*

---

*All but **11** make a giant bed for **11** to lie in (**7**, **13** and **16** stand as the headboard, others kneel, facing each other with arms outstretched).*

13   I finally fall asleep deeply, deeply unhappy that Grandad doesn't really have Arsehammers and can't really transport himself and just turn up –

7 + 16   Kaboom!

13   – anywhere.

11   Grandad isn't going to save the world with the other Grandads and Grandmas and Experts.

13   Grandad is just plain Grandad and he is old.

11   Sometimes, I decide, I just don't like my mum.

Scene 13: Grandad Says Goodbye

7, 13, 16   Later that night I am woken by a loud clatter and a thump.

All   I sit bolt upright.

2 + 9   There, at the foot of my bed, stands Grandad.

All *look at the same agreed, fixed point in theatre.*

10 + 15   While I watch with amazement, Grandad stands tall and proud,

4 + 12   clicks his heels together,

3 + 14   salutes and bellows triumphantly,

Grandad   (*voice on tape*) 'Arsehammers!'

5 + 8   Then, with a smile and a wink,

7, 13, 16   Grandad disappears.

11   I stop sulking.

---

7   The next morning Mum tells me that Grandad has died peacefully in the night.

+16   She tells Claudia that Grandad has gone to live with the angels.

+4   Later that afternoon I tell Claudia that there are no such things as angels

+12   and that Grandad has simply arsehammered his way back

+3   to live with Grandma.

All Kaboom!

Scene 14: Epilogue and Tableau

Everyone sits at the feet of **1**, *who is using the dice as a 'podium'.*

1 *Sings 'We'll Meet Again' unaccompanied.*

All cast collect toys and return to original squares from Scene 1.

At end of song, repeat of individual scenarios from Music 1.

All freeze.

The Year of the Monkey

Adapted by Liz Light

This version of *The Year of the Monkey* was first produced by **Stage2** at the Crescent Theatre, Birmingham, on 12 January 2011 with the following cast and creatives:

Bride's Side
Rose, *Mother of the Bride* — Charlie Reilly

Sarah, *Bride* — Katie Booth
Matron of Honour — Emma Staunton
Bridesmaid 1 — Daisy Ilic
Bridesmaid 2 — Rosa Simonet

Tom, *Father of the Bride* — Ethan Hudson
Jonathan, *Brother of the Bride* — Jonni Dowsett
Grandfather of the Bride — Alex Butler

Ist Friend (*of Rose*) — Hannah Scott
Julia (*Friend of Rose*) — Elin Dowsett
Beautiful — Rosie Nisbet
Lovely — Sandra Peters
Marvellous — Helen Carter

Groom's Side
Steven, *Groom* — Neil Gardner
Best Man — Abel Graham

Beatrice, *Mother of the Groom* — Siobhan Twissell*
Jack, *Father of the Groom* — Sam Hotchin

Groom's Friend 1 — Bernie O'Toole
Groom's Friend 2 — Sarah Mooney

Other
Vicar — Katie Snape
Photographer — Annabel Smith**
DJ — Ethan Tarr
Waitress 1 — Sophie Bowser
Waitress 2 — Ella Otomewo

Fred the Stranger — Connor Fox

Crew
Director Liz Light
Assistant Director/Line Allocations Annabel Smith
Production Manager/Lighting Designer Chris Cuthbert
Lighting Operator Tom Booth
Sound Operator Ryan Fox
Backstage Manager Alex Pugh
Head Chaperone Lucy Bailey-Wright

Production revived on 25th February at The Dovehouse Theatre for the **2011 BDTG FAME Festival**, with the following cast changes
*Chloe Jones
**George Hannigan

The Alexandra Theatre Trophy for Best Adult One Act Play
Winner

The William DS Bennett Trophy for Direction
Winner – Liz Light

The Rose Bowl for Any Outstanding Achievement in an Adult One Act Play
Winner – The Antiphonal Prayer Scene in *The Year of the Monkey*
Nominated – The 'Musical Chairs' sequence in *The Year of the Monkey*

The Bert Newton Trophy for Technical Achievement
Nominated – for Costume
Nominated – for Lighting and Sound

The Herringshaw Trophy for Most Outstanding Male Adult Performance
Nominated and Highly Commended – Connor Fox (Fred the Stranger)

The Noele Gordon Trophy for Most Outstanding Female Adult Performance
Nominated – Charlie Reilly (Rose)

Preset

A 5m × 5m square with 20 stools arranged in rows, with an aisle leading to a 5-chair altar.

No-one on stage for first atmospheric song.

Music

Irish folk music for 'Thoughts' scenes and relevant music – ie 1st Dance for 'Wedding' scenes.

Costume

All in black, white, grey and green – relevant to roles at the wedding.

Characters

Bride's Side
Rose, *Mother of the Bride*
Sarah, *Bride*
Matron of Honour
Bridesmaid 1
Bridesmaid 2
Tom, *Father of the Bride*
Jonathan, *Brother of the Bride*
Grandfather of the Bride
Ist Friend (*of Rose*)
Julia (*Friend of Rose*)
Beautiful
Lovely
Marvellous

Groom's Side
Steven, *Groom*
Best Man
Beatrice, *Mother of the Groom*
Jack, *Father of the Groom*
Groom's Friend 1
Groom's Friend 2

Other
Vicar
Photographer
DJ
Waitress 1
Waitress 2
Fred the Stranger

Scene 1: Dark Days   **Thoughts**

Characters enter on their lines and take their logical places in a church facing the altar.

Rose   There are dark days.

Tom   And sometimes the dark days turn into dark nights

Vicar   and you wake up in dark days again.

Steven   And one thing leads to another,

Best Man   each blacker than before

Grandfather   till you swear that the blindness is permanent.

Jonathan   But somewhere inside you,

Matron of Honour   you hope to find the light switch,

Beatrice   even though nine-tenths of you is saying there isn't one,

Jack   and nine out of ten people are saying you aren't blind anyway.

Julia   So you struggle in vain

1st Friend   and in dark days.

Sarah   And all around the noise from the neighbours is deafening,

Groom's Friend 1   increasing the isolation.

Groom's Friend 2   Blind and deaf, deaf and blind,

Beautiful   how to communicate,

Marvellous   how to be part of things when you're blind and deaf?

Bridesmaid 1   You can't see and you can't hear

Photographer   but someone, somewhere,

DJ   out of the goodness of their heart

Fred   is building wheelchair ramps.

Lovely   But don't complain

Bridesmaid 2   or you might be seen as ungrateful,

Waitress 1   even though in not complaining you are struck dumb.

Waitress 2   Blind, deaf and dumb.

All   The year of the monkey.

Scene 2: Procession Down the Aisle   Wedding

Vicar   A wedding.

Rose   My daughter.

Vicar   But weddings.

1st Friend   Aren't you proud, Rose? She looks beautiful!

Matron of Honour   Beautiful, yes. And so she should. We went to five different shops.

Bridesmaid 1   She must've tried on hundreds of dresses, my feet were killing me, trailing around back and forth,

Bridesmaid 2   and you know what? She finally decided on the one she saw first.

Matron of Honour   Typical, isn't it? So difficult, trying to get it right.

Rose   I wasn't needed though.

Matron of Honour   Sarah has a mind of her own, a very independent young lady.

Rose   I went because she asked.

Bridesmaid 1   She asked because it's the done thing.

Rose   I wanted to be needed, I think Sarah wanted to need me,

Matron of Honour   but in the end I was just company,

Bridesmaid 2   somebody to nod or frown when asked,

Sarah   What do you think?

Matron of Honour   My function to second-guess whether she expected a nod or a frown.

Bridesmaid 1   Get it wrong and I'd become a burden, a hindrance.

Bridesmaid 2   Get it right and the mother/daughter scenario's complete.

Rose   I'm well practised in getting things right.

Rose   A helix.

+ Sarah   A double helix

+ Bridesmaid 2   like a DNA strand.

+ Bridesmaid 1   Merging and twirling

+ Matron of Honour   and

Tom   completing each other.

Scene 3: God and Counsellor   Thoughts

Rose   The church. I like churches.

Grandfather   Go into the church while it's empty,

Julia   before the next wedding.

Beautiful   Cool, echoing, forbidding.

Fred   They're supposed to be welcoming, these lonely places.

Lovely   The vicar saying,

Vicar   Can I help you, Madam?

Rose   Just wanted a quiet word with the Lord, vicar.

Vicar   Oh, of course, of course.

Rose   Idiot.

Waitress 1   Wouldn't talk to God,

Waitress 2   what's God going to do?

DJ   It's like talking to a counsellor.

Groom's Friend 2   They just sit benignly while you burble on, a half smile or look of concern,

Jack   or pass the man-size tissues, delete where applicable.

Best Man   They don't do anything.

Tom   In the end you solve your own problems, usually by swallowing hard and learning to live with it.

Rose   I can't even remember now why Tom and I went.

Jonathan   Mid-life crisis, I expect.

1st Friend + Marvellous   No, it was more than that.

Photographer   It started years before.

Rose   I couldn't explain.

Groom's Friend 1   Can't explain feelings to people who don't feel them.

Beatrice   It was after Jonathan was born . . .

Jonathan   Empty, aloof,

Rose   I keep feeding him food

Jonathan   but it isn't enough.

Rose   I play with him,

1st Friend   watch him,

Marvellous   nurture him,

1st Friend + Marvellous   bathe him,

Rose   but I don't know how to take him into this feeling.

Photographer   It's almost sensual but deeper.

Groom's Friend 1   A natural, right feeling that's locked away in my inadequacy to express it.

Beatrice   Start resenting the feeling because I can't use it,

Rose   can't get it out of me,

Jonathan   everything else goes grey.

Jonathan, 1st Friend, Marvellous, Photographer, Groom's Friend 1, Beatrice   Mother's death was the exact opposite but exactly the same.

Jonathan   The connection.

Rose   I never realised it till then.

1st Friend, Marvellous, Photographer, Groom's Friend 1, Beatrice   In all those years we never touched that deeply. And her death made it too late.

Grandfather   Must be some way of being on time.

Scene 4: Watching the Ceremony   Wedding

*Volume switches between actual Wedding Ceremony (represented by lines in **bold**), and guest reactions.*

LOUD (Focus)   QUIET (Background)

Vicar   **Steven, will you take Sarah to be your wife?**

Bridesmaid 1	Sarah's a social climber,
Bridesmaid 2	a career girl.

Vicar **Will you love her, comfort her, honour and protect her, and, forsaking all others, be faithful to her as long as you both shall live?**

Steven **I will.**

Vicar **Sarah, will you take Steven to be your husband?**

Rose	I don't understand her.
Bridesmaid 1	She wears shoulder pads
Bridesmaid 2	and bright red lipstick,
Matron of Honour	and might – *'might'* – have children in her mid-thirties,
Steven	possibly, if everything's *'on track'*

Vicar **Will you love him, comfort him, honour and protect him, and, forsaking all others, be faithful to him as long as you both shall live?**

Sarah **I will.**

Vicar **Will you, the family and friends of Steven and Sarah, support and uphold them in their marriage now and in the years to come?**

All	**We will.**		
Vicar	**Steven and Sarah, I now invite you to join hands and make your vows, in the presence of God and his people.**		
Steven	**I, Steven, take you, Sarah, To be my wife**		
Matron of Honour	There are no creases in her clothes	**Steven**	**To have and to hold**
			From this day forward;
			For better, for worse,
			For richer, for poorer,
Best Man	and I've got a sneaking suspicion this wedding is a career move.		**In sickness and in health,**
			To love and to cherish,
			Till death us do part;
			According to God's holy law
Steven	**In the presence of God I make this vow.**		
Sarah	**I, Sarah, take you, Steven, To be my husband**		

Rose	I've done it,	**Sarah**	**To have and to hold**
Tom	I made it happen.		**From this day forward;**
Bridesmaid 1	A homemaker,		**For better, for worse,**
Bridesmaid 2	housewife,		**For richer, for poorer,**
Rose	mother,		**In sickness and in health,**
Matron of Honour	drumming good table manners,		**To love and to cherish,**
Bridesmaid 1	please		**Till death us do part;**
Bridesmaid 2	and thank you,		**According to God's holy law**

Vicar	**In the presence of God and before this congregation,**
Matron of Honour	and never let the neighbours know your business.
Vicar	And if you're taken for granted it's because your efforts were seamless. **You may now kiss the bride.**

Scene 5: I'd Rather Be In Bed!   **Thoughts**

Rose   I'm everything I'm not.

Photographer   I'm everything I could have been.

DJ   I lie in bed and lead myself up the garden path.

Photographer   But not just in bed.

DJ   Not any more.

Rose   Just bed's easiest,

Photographer   no having to excuse myself,

DJ   explain myself,

Photographer   beg anybody's pardon

DJ   or hope to bluff.

Photographer   Bed's easiest,

DJ   bed's where it started.

Photographer + DJ   Concentration's difficult, that's the point.

Rose   I have to struggle to concentrate because really I'd rather be napping.

Scene 6: Grandparents   **Wedding**

Matron of Honour   And then back outside,

Best Man   back to the sunshine

Rose   and my father. I'm sorry, Dad, were you waiting?

Grandfather   It's all right, Rose, I'm in no hurry. And Jonathan's kept me company. I like to sit, pause occasionally.

Jonathan   Pause? Nap.

Grandfather   Feel it.

Rose   And then he says,

Grandfather   I was thinking about your mother, Rose. It's a pity she missed it.

Rose   Jonathan says,

Jonathan   She was here, Grandad, in all our thoughts. Didn't you feel her?

Rose   She was here, Jonathan felt her, Jonathan was napping.

Scene 7: Boring Family Life   **Thoughts**

Groom's Friend 1 + Groom's Friend 2   And God, we're so comfortable, aren't we, all of us.

Photographer, DJ, Matron of Honour, Best Man   It's what we worked for,

Tom, 1st Friend, Julia   the ground plan that was laid . . . when?

Beatrice, Jack   Probably by our parents.

Vicar, Sarah, Steven   Striving to be so comfortable,

Bridesmaid 1 + Bridesmaid 2   to have no worries,

Waitress 1 + Waitress 2   no adversity,

Beautiful, Marvellous, Lovely   then putting on party frocks and muttering banal epithets because our lives are so lacking in . . .

Grandfather   depth.

Scene 8: Photographs   **Wedding**

Throughout first part of scene, **photographer** *sets formal group shots.*

Photographer   Photographs. Smile! Say cheese!

Rose   Why don't you have an Irish wedding, Sarah?

Sarah   Because we're not Irish, Mother.

Grandfather   Oh, I'm sure there's a bit of Irish in us somewhere, there's a bit of Irish in everybody.

Matron of Honour   We could whirl and twirl and drink and yeehaa!

Bridesmaid 1   . . . We could get dizzy

Bridesmaid 2   . . . We could get drunk

Best Man   . . . We could get sentimental.

DJ   When Irish eyes are smiling . . .

Beatrice   It's not done.

Jack   We're English.

Julia   We don't have the emotional licence.

Groom's Friend 1 + Groom's Friend 2   It's noisy.

Beautiful   Crowded.

Marvellous   Drunken.

Lovely   Messy.

Rose   Too much like fun.

Thoughts

Everyone in final full group shot for model family portrait, but scene morphs into drunken chaos.

Photographer   Come on, people, smile!

Tom   Oh, me poor wee darlin'.

Waitress 1, Waitress 2, Groom's Friend 1, Groom's Friend 2   Touralouraloura . . .

Jonathan   Oh, mammy, I'm gonna miss you.

Grandfather   Oh, Danny boy . . .

1st Friend   And isn't your poor daddy weeping buckets over you, even though you'll be moving in next door?

Sarah   I'm dancing! I'm flying!

Rose   No. Enjoyment is for people who don't deserve success.

Scene 9: I Hate TV and Suburbia   **Thoughts**

Rose   I watch TV but I hate it, it's so unrealistic. Every programme is dramatic, something happening, people in the middle of some big crisis.

Groom's Friend 2   Life's not like that. Even the documentaries which are supposed to be true, they're all about trauma, conflict, always somebody in tears.

Groom's Friend 1   Nothing ever happens,

Groom's Friend 2   or rarely.

Rose   Tom and I,

Tom   we've worked to be secure, strived to avoid all drama, tragedy, as much as possible

Grandfather   the occasional death in the family, naturally,

Jonathan   but even that's been expected.

Rose   Of course I don't want tragedy.

Half of Cast (*except* Rose) – Left of Stage   Hate the pain of conflict

Half of Cast (*except* Rose) – Right of Stage   – everybody does

Rose   – but . . .

Groom's Friend 1   And who do we hate?

Groom's Friend 2   Who do we fear?

Lovely   Ourselves.

Steven   Hate our emotions.

Tom   Fear expressing our emotions.

Beatrice   And hate and fear

Waitress 2   those with nothing to lose.

Julia   People who dress differently,

Matron of Honour   act differently,

Best Man   whose priorities are not comfortable,

Marvellous   middle class,

Vicar   humdrum,

Jack   wall-to-wall,

Beautiful   centrally heated

Rose   tedium.

Bridesmaid 1   People with spirit,

Photographer   people with things to fight for.

1st Friend   To fight against us,

DJ   to fight back

Grandfather   because we demand they join

Waitress 1   or suffer our march for comfort.

Bridesmaid 2   A comfort that stifles

Jonathan   and bores us

Sarah   but God forbid we should ever let it go.

Fred   God forbid

Rose   we should do something more useful than arranging jumble sales for the NSPCC.

Scene 10: Stepford Friends   **Wedding**

Wedding guests travel along family line up, congratulating and greeting as appropriate.

Jack   Have to content ourselves with clumsy hugs

Beatrice   and quick pecks on cheeks.

Beautiful   She looks beautiful.

Lovely   A lovely do.

Marvellous   Marvellous day for it.

All wedding guests ad lib. around the words 'beautiful, lovely, marvellous', building in momentum and volume until . . .

Scene 11: Shut Up Stupid People   Thoughts

Rose   Oh, shut up, you stupid people!

1st Friend   Did the power of speech evolve for this?

Julia   To be controlled, to be gagged by etiquette, manners?

1st Friend   The middle classes, invented as guardians of social conventions?

Julia   Ensuring that nobody aspires to anything greater than knowing how to behave in public?

All   How very kind.

All wedding guests circulate using the words 'how very kind' until a fixed point.

Scene 12: The Reception   Wedding

Family members from both sides sit across top table. Three other tables seat four guests each. **Fred** *sits alone. Waitresses on shift.*

Waitress 1 + Waitress 2   And the reception.

Beatrice   What an expense,

Jack   What a waste.

Rose   Doing this because everybody else does it.

Tom   And if we didn't do it?

Jonathan   If Sarah didn't think it was important?

Steven   If Sarah didn't think it was guaranteed to make the day special,

Sarah   make you enjoy it,

Steven   the happiest day of your life,

Rose   and then feel oh so guilty because it's not?

Grandfather   We don't know how to enjoy ourselves anymore,

Matron of Honour   follow rules,

Best Man   told how it's done

Matron of Honour   how it should be done.

Rose   The only thing wrong is that everybody feels the same

+ Grandfather   but is afraid of saying.

Rose   Beatrice, Jack? I do hope you're enjoying the do?

Beatrice   Oh, absolutely, you and Tom have worked wonders.

Jack   Wonders.

Rose   We should be soaring, flying, leaping this social barbed wire of struggling to find words innocuous enough to remain polite.

Tom   Of friendly

Rose   meaningless

Tom   chit-chat.

Scene 13: I Want Passion   Thoughts

Rose   God, I want some passion, some drama. I want Steven to have jilted her at the altar.

Steven   She'd have crumbled,

All (*except* **Rose**)   the crowd would have muttered, gossip, tittle-tattle,

Bridesmaid 2   Sarah would have folded into her dress,

Bridesmaid 1   creased

Bridesmaid 2   and weeping,

Rose   and I'd have been there.

Grandfather   Tom would've twitched, paced, backed off,

Jonathan   unable to take control, unable to fix it

Rose   and I'd have been there, flying in, reliable,

Tom   sympathising, comforting, the one she needed,

Rose   the one she's always needed.

All (*except* **Rose**)   Touralouraloura . . .

Beatrice   Nothing to celebrate. Mothers are never allowed to take part in celebrations.

Jack   Pretend to be important, look good, stay in the background or the kitchen.

Rose   Drama though, crisis.

Fred   Step forward two paces and take control.

Rose   We've strived to avoid it, Tom and I.

Jonathan   But what if Jonathan had been a drug addict?

Photographer   And then there's Tom.

DJ   The relationship with him,

Photographer   not knowing what it means,

DJ   not quite able to grasp the undercurrent so easily.

Photographer   Tom saying,

Tom   God I felt so proud, leading her down the aisle. She looks beautiful doesn't she?

Beautiful   Beautiful,

Lovely   lovely,

Marvellous   marvellous.

Rose   Tom.

1st Friend + Julia   More like genetic engineering,

Rose   a man-made double helix,

Julia   half natural,

1st Friend   half built.

1st Friend + Julia   Maybe even two separate ones,

Julia   which just happen to turn at the same rhythm.

1st Friend   A strange emotional complexity.

Rose   Tom.

Beatrice   Hanging on, on the outside, the periphery, the way men do.

Jack   Wanting to enter, trying to enter,

Beatrice   but somehow not quite making it, sometimes giving up, retreating,

Jack   sometimes trying even harder.

Scene 14: Start of Tom's Speech   Wedding

Tom *prepares to give formal 'Father of the Bride Speech.'*

Vicar   And the speeches.

Rose   Tom's speech.

Tom   Unaccustomed as I am to making speeches. Or rather getting a word in edgeways when the wife is in the vicinity.

All (*except* **Rose**)   Ha ha ha.

Scene 15: *I* **Want to Make a Speech**   **Thoughts**

Tom *is usurped.*

Tom   A speech.

Rose   I want to make a speech.

Sarah + Steven   I want to be there.

Vicar, Beautiful, Marvellous, Lovely, Fred   Unaccustomed as I am to blowing my own trumpet and making my voice heard

Bridesmaid 2, Photographer, Groom's Friend 1, Groom's Friend 2   I'd just like to say to hell with the notion of traditional weddings, to hell with the archaic giving the daughter away from one man to the other,

1st Friend, Julia, Bridesmaid 1, DJ   father of the bride, walking down the aisle, big important honcho, while mother wears a hat and weeps.

Jonathan, Grandfather, Beatrice, Jack, Best Man, Matron of Honour   I would like to make a speech for a change.

Rose   I would

DJ   like to speak as the ever vigilant one,

Photographer   who lived daily, constantly with the chaos

Lovely   and battle of clashing desires.

Rose   I was

Groom's Friend 2   the one who struggled,

1st Friend   often for a full ten minutes,

Vicar   to put a pair of Clarks on a wriggling one-year-old,

Rose   I was

Bridesmaid 2   the one who had to deal with the kicking and screaming temper tantrum

Julia   of a seven-year-old in the middle of Marks and Spencers

Marvellous   over something as simple as the word 'no' to a chocolate Santa.

Rose   I was

Beautiful   the one who had to bear the brunt of a scowling fourteen-year-old

Bridesmaid 1   loudly declaring her undying hatred of me in a seaside café in Bournemouth.

Rose   I am

Fred   the one who lives daily with deep powerful affection

Groom's Friend 1   for the memory of resented times.

Rose   And I don't want to be the one

+ Beatrice + Jack   who sits silently, in stupid frock and frightful hat,

+ Grandfather   while my daughter experiences one of the most important events of her life!

+ Matron of Honour   I love her. I hope she'll be happy

+ Best Man   and I think Steven is a wonderful man.

+ Jonathan   I wish them all the best.

+ everyone else   Thank you.

Rose   Did I or didn't I?

Scene 16: Rest of Tom's Speech   Wedding

Waitress 2   Tom's successful.

Waitress 1   Tom feels successful,

Waitress 2   but he's woken every morning by an alarm clock, ordered by a little piece of plastic machinery to move himself.

Waitress 1   Most times he doesn't want to get up,

Waitress 2   most times he wants to roll over, forget about life,

Waitress 1   but the alarm clock's the boss,

Waitress 2   the alarm clock's in charge.

Waitress 1   Even if he ignored the alarm clock he'd feel guilty,

Waitress 2   feel he ought to obey.

Waitress 1 + Waitress 2   And they say man rules the earth.

Tom   Fathers and daughters, it is said, have a special relationship . . .

Scene 17: Tom's Changed But I Want Drama   Thoughts

Rose   Either he's changed or I have, I don't know which.

Tom   There's nothing wrong,

Rose   nothing I can put my finger on.

1st Friend   It seems to be a steady hum of daily routine.

Groom's Friend 1   No point in leaving for that.

Matron of Honour   No point in leaving because someone's kind, considerate, willing.

Beautiful   Because I feel somehow disengaged.

Julia   Because I prefer it when he's not there,

Best Man   because when he's there I think,

Rose   get out, go away, get out of my house.

Vicar   I want something else, something more.

Lovely   Something more than this dull,

Photographer   throbbing sense of resentment about . . . what?

Marvellous   The inability to connect?

Groom's Friend 2   To howl together?

1st Friend   I don't feel in step,

Groom's Friend 1   still feel like a youngster,

Matron of Honour   waiting to start, waiting for it all to make sense.

Beautiful   And I see Tom getting old

Julia   and I realise my time's been wasted, used up.

Best Man   Spent my life preparing for life,

Vicar   spent my life waiting for life.

Lovely   I don't think anything will change by throwing everything up in the air and starting again.

Rose   It's the 'underneath it all',

Marvellous   I want the underneath it all,

Groom's Friend 2   I just want to feel it. Be there.

DJ   It's happening again, can't control it.

Matron of Honour   I want to stay, talk to these people,

Marvellous   concentrate, stay fixed, firm, can't.

Bridesmaid 2   I want something to happen.

Photographer   I want something that I know is happening.

Grandfather   I want Jonathan to be a drug addict,

Jonathan   a known drug addict.

Groom's Friend 2   I want everybody on their toes,

Lovely   waiting for something to go hideously wrong.

Jonathan   Jonathan upending the tables in some mad psychotic outburst,

Sarah   Sarah wailing, her day thoroughly ruined.

Tom   Tom, exasperated, embarrassed, trying to control him, ending up fighting.

Steven   Steven joining in like the new dutiful son in law.

Bridesmaid 1   Chairs strewn clumsily aside,

Best Man   food flying, guests in chaos,

Groom's Friend 1   their hats comically askew.

Julia   Marzipan icing smeared on their best suits,

Vicar   silk ties ruined by hurled red wine,

Rose   everybody shouting

All   oh my goodness!

1st Friend   Practical women frenziedly collecting knives,

Beautiful   bottles and glasses,

Jack   in case things turn bloody.

Rose   And amidst it all I hit you all, I smack you generously round the face

Tom   for daring to say what you're supposed to say,

Sarah + Steven   what it's done to say,

Rose   I look you squarely in the eyes and shout . . .

All   Speak up! Tell me what you're feeling!

Jack   Take that stupid hat off and blow your top!

Rose   We'd have something to talk about then, be a part of each other's feelings.

Scene 18: Wedding Dances   **Wedding**

Bride *and* **Groom** *dance to song of their choice.*

Music and dance continue to underscore the scene.

Rose   Jonathan says

Jonathan   to you, Mum, you've worked wonders.

Rose   Wonders? The wedding or the outburst?

Jonathan   The wedding,

Rose   he's talking about the wedding. He's talking about weeks, not years.

DJ   Sssh. A time and a place for everything they say,

Rose   all the time in the world to talk about nothing.

Rose   Julia! How nice to see you.

Julia   Rose! How are you?

Rose   Fine. So glad you could make it. Hate this strain,

Julia   find it such hard work.

Rose   Heard it all before.

Beautiful   Same people,

Marvellous   same sentences,

Lovely   put on their party frocks,

1st Friend   party faces,

Julia   and do their party pieces.

Matron of Honour   And they're doing it today for Sarah.

Rose, Tom, Grandfather, Jonathan   Because Sarah's going when I don't really know her,

Beatrice   when we've lived this superficial relationship

Jack   and ignored the churning undercurrents.

Best Man   Disregarded

Matron of Honour   the bubbling emotions

1st Friend, Julia, Beautiful, Lovely, Marvellous   because it's not done to talk about them.

All   Because now's not the time, now's never the time.

Rose   All the time in the world to talk about nothing.

Scene 19: Funerals   **Thoughts**

*Family members (**Tom**, **Sarah**, **Jonathan**, **Grandfather**) sitting on pews/chairs in centre.*

Rose *and* **Fred** *in back row, furthest from altar (and* **Vicar***), but closest to audience.*

Group A sitting in a line down one side, all lines whispered.

(Bridesmaid 1, **Bridesmaid 2**, **Matron of Honour**, **1st Friend**, **Julia**, **Beautiful**, **Lovely**, **Marvellous**, **Photographer**)

Group B sitting in a line down the other, all lines whispered.

(Steven, **Best Man**, **Beatrice**, **Jack**, **DJ**, **Waitress 1**, **Waitress 2**, **Groom's Friend 1**, **Groom's Friend 2**)

Rose   People always interrupt. I suppose I don't mind today.

Fred   Funerals, though, I get incensed when people interrupt at funerals.

Vicar   Funerals are different.

Rose   I'm always wary at funerals. Practicality is my middle name, on the outside.

Fred   But inside my mind's awash with thoughts of ghosts and reincarnation and . . . and something, something spiritual, something other-worldly, something the scientists dismiss as mere chemical combination.

Vicar   God?

Rose   No.

Fred   Not the religious God anyway.

Group A   Not the anthropomorphic God.

Group B   Not sermons and holy books and thou shalts and shalt nots.

Group A   It's something other,

Group B   something else,

Group A   something to do with pre-sleep

Group B   and strolling

Sarah + Jonathan   and double helix children.

Grandfather   Totally natural yet unnervingly profound.

Vicar   Funerals –

Rose   if I concentrate, if nobody interrupts –

Fred   funerals have the same atmosphere, the same potential.

Rose   I go to funerals now.

Fred   It's a hobby.

Rose   I sit quietly at the back.

Fred   There's another man.

Rose   I see him quite regularly,

Fred   I think it's a hobby with him too. We don't speak, just nod.

Rose   Nobody seems to mind.

Fred   The atmosphere, I can feel it. The dead aren't dead, they're hovering, reading our emotions, feeling us.

Rose   When mother died,

Grandfather   the helix broken.

Rose   My connection to her wrenched away,

Grandfather   stamped underfoot in one swift movement.

Rose   And I never said. I never asked if she felt it too –

Fred   till the funeral.

Group A   Till the funeral when I felt her there,

Group B   felt her hovering,

Group A   felt her trying to repair the helix,

Rose   both of us desperately trying to reconnect,

Group A   pushing towards each other,

Group B   struggling to reunite,

Group A   to feel that feeling again,

Group B   that feeling that was never properly celebrated.

Group A   Never acknowledged fully, taken for granted, ignored

Group B   while lesser, trivial, meaningless nothingness was
pursued.

Vicar   People don't interrupt at funerals.

Rose   There are things we never said, Mother.

All (*except* **Rose**)   Things we never needed to say.

Rose   Didn't we?

All (*except* **Rose**)   We knew them, really, both of us. Besides
which, Rose, it was the feelings that counted.

Rose   Yes, but did we each know what the other was feeling?

All (*except* **Rose**)   Underneath it all, we did.

Sarah   Underneath it all.

Jonathan   Underneath it all.

Rose   Underneath it all's not good enough.

Tom   Underneath it all lasts a lifetime and what's the point of spending your whole life keeping your true feelings underneath it all?

All (*except* **Rose**)   Oh, Rose, you worry too much. Does a DNA strand ever unravel and separate?

Grandfather   Only when you're dead.

Rose   I think it's me. I feel it at funerals.

Fred   Sat at the back on my own, the man in the other aisle. We always sit in adjacent aisles. Fred

Rose   I call him,

Fred   Fred the stranger.

Rose   We never speak,

Fred   just nod, a half smile suiting the occasion.

Rose   It would spoil it if we spoke,

Fred   we both know.

Rose   Funny how disappointed I feel when he's not there.

Group A   The pit of the stomach, brimming with emotion, uncontrolled, animal, sexual,

Group B   wading in mud and feeling. Deep, deep howling.

Rose   I couldn't take Tom,

Group B   couldn't even tell Tom.

Group A   Tell him I'm going for a walk,

Group B   he hates walking too,

Rose   so I'm safe he'll never join me.

Grandfather   Tom would say,

Tom   What do you want to go to other people's funerals for? You never even knew them.

Fred   He doesn't understand.

Rose   Because the atmosphere, Tom, the atmosphere is reeling with emotion,

Fred   collective loneliness concentrating our minds in on ourselves.

Group A   We're all there, disparate human beings, different characters, personalities, lives

Group B   and we're all feeling our solitude, together, wordlessly, honestly

Group A   and muttering pleasantries is the hardest thing,

Group B   muttering pleasantries is unnecessary,

Group A   because nothing needs to be said,

Group B   it's all felt.

Fred   Underneath we're all dogs howling at the moon.

Rose   Fred the stranger howls, I know he does,

Vicar   it's why he's there.

Scene 20: Double Helix is Two Words   Wedding

Rose   I asked Sarah if she was enjoying her day and she said,

Sarah   yes, of course.

Rose   Then she added,

Sarah   a bit sad too, in a way.

Rose   And I hugged her and said, double helix. Don't you just love that word?

Sarah   That's two words, Mum.

Rose   Exactly. My point entirely. Touralouraloura.

Scene 21: Napping Alone   Thoughts

Grooms Friend 1   A helix.

Groom's Friend 2   A double helix

Beautiful   like a DNA strand.

Marvellous   Merging and twirling

Lovely   and completing each other.

Rose   That's how I feel when I touch her.

Tom   My son too.

Jonathan   Jonathan and Sarah,

Sarah   Sarah and Jonathan.

Waitress 1   My children.

Waitress 2   Touching my children.

Grandfather   They're grown now, gone.

Beatrice   And the house is finished

Best Man   so I nap.

Matron of Honour   A quiet stroll down the country lanes of my mind

Jack   I like to call it,

Julia   when I'm feeling pretentious.

1st Friend   Mostly, however, I call it a nap,

Vicar   although actual sleep has nothing to do with it.

Fred   It's the before sleep, pre-sleep.

Bridesmaid 1   Wandering off, strolling.

Bridesmaid 2   Escaping this world,

DJ   this life of social graces and béchamel sauce

Photographer   and the occasional flap of a wedding or anniversary.

Rose   A church. A wedding. My daughter's. I'm not really there, miles away, napping.

Hard Working Families

Dedicated to Liz Light and all at **Stage2**, *with thanks for their inspiration.*

Hard Working Families was first produced by **Stage2** at the Crescent Theatre, Birmingham, on 7 January 2016 with the following cast and creatives:

Grandad	Dan Nash
Natalie	Violette Townsend-Sprigg
Natalie's Mum	Izzy Jones Rigby
Dennis	Amit Mevorach
Dennis's Mum	Rosie Nisbet

Natalie's Friends: **Dennis's Friends**:

Lily	Georgie Nott	**George**	Toma Hoffman
	Lizzy Broderick		Reuben Jones Rigby
	Daisy Wilkes		Dillan McKeever
	Carmen Hutchins		Louis Delaney
	Ellie Waide		Fabio Sula

Politician	Emily Cremins
Politician's Secretary	Laura Dowsett
Politician's PR Assistant	Roni Mevorach
A & E Worker	Maya Bennett
Postman	Aldora Lekgegaj
Banker	Hana Ali
Boss	Jacob Otomewo
Dog Shelter Volunteer	Teigan Jones
Gas Board Worker	Hanifa Ali
Nanny	Megan Fisher
Au Pair	Alice Nott
Gardener	Matt Levesley
Cleaner	Soph Adilypour
Job Centre Worker	Meg Luesley
Tap Shoes Mum	Emma Watson
Disabled Son's Dad	Karam Johal
Placard Holder	Brianna Whitty
Tailor	Tabitha Green
Doctor	Katelyn Stephenson
Mr Showbiz	Jack Deakin
Contestant 1	Robert Fretwell
Contestant 2	Kloe Vincent

Unlucky Brian   Toby Jowitt, Jacob Rose
Vicki/Lovely Assistant 1   Tia Forbes
Violette/Lovely Assistant 2   Pippa Nisbet
Veriti/Lovely Assistant 3   Chloe Jennings
Tom   Ben Lawrence-Pietroni
Dick   Charlie Stewart
Harry   Jack Barton
Fishing Boy   Hemal Pallan
Boarding School Girl   Eva Williams
Maths Boy   Luke Rowbottom
Timetable Girl   Josie Rowbottom
Miranda   Lilya Datta
David   Dylan Datta

Band
Keyboards Charlie Reilly
Guitar Mark James
Bass George Mee
Drums Alex Earle

Chorus

Jasmine Davis	Adriana Ruttledge	Kiah McPherson
Rebecca Holmes	Lele Samms	Blair Natty-Brown
Toby Jowitt	Vrindavani Dasa	Vinnie Pollet
Daniel McCloskey	Joel Fleming	Jacob Rose
Murriam Murtaza	Sarina Johal	Sebastian Sanders
Kairo Palmer	Alfie McMillan	Corey White

Advert 1

Kate Goodall	Rose Gordon	Debbie Harrison
Sean Waide	Al Hutchins	Joy Levesley
Astrid Voigt	Tracy Vincent	
Toma Hoffman	Eva Williams	

Advert 2

Gerard Lekgegaj	Ramsay Hutchins	Toby Painter
Roma Pallan	Oscar Strong	Lily Cunney
Audrey Reinarz	Lucie Stephenson	Indigo Perrett
Blair Natty-Brown	Felix Lawrence-Pietroni	

Advert 3

Chloe Jones	Khalid Daley	Hemal Pallan

Crew

Director Liz Light
Production Manager Ethan Hudson
Lighting Designer Will Monks
Musical Director Charlie Reilly
Lighting Operator Luca Hoffman
Sound Operator Bradley Layton
Technical Assistant Tom Barber
Costume Assistant Laura Dowsett
Stage Manager Kloe Vincent
Production Assistants Jack Deakin, Radelina Ancheva
Advert Directors Mark James, Charlie Reilly
Cinematography Alex Earle
Scenic Artist Alexander Butler
Backstage Manager Katie Booth
Chaperones Sarah Kemp, Sarah Middlemiss

Characters

Natalie + friends
Natalie's mum
Dennis + friends
Dennis's mum
Politician + aides
Grandad
Game Show Host
Vicki, Veriti and Violette / Lovely Assistants
Tom, Dick and Harry

CHORUS takes on all other roles including:

Boss. A&E Worker. Postman. Banker. Gas Worker. Gardener. Cleaner. Job Centre Worker. Union Rep. Dog Volunteer. Nanny. Au Pair. Unlucky Brian. David. Miranda.

Most of the **Chorus** roles can be doubled or tripled.

Script includes additional scene and line allocations by Liz Light and Charlie Reilly for original **Stage2** production.

Lines in italics possibly sung – though not songs as such.

Act One

Preset

Giant pound coins, used to play games, as furniture, props, as anything and everything possible. Whole set covered in 'money', blown up pictures of 10, 20, 50 pound notes, coins etc.

Buzzer or Klaxon sounds.

Cast and Chorus all enter singing:

> *Money is above me*
> *Money comes before me*
> *It is worth more than me*
> *I am worth less. (Repeat till alarm.)*

An alarm goes off – definite early morning clock alarm.

Music: Housemartins – Sheep.

Everybody running around frantically getting ready for work, school etc. **Natalie**'s *family moving slower, interacting with each other in a friendly, close way. Some playing parents, others kids, some single, childless, showing the difference and/or similarity in day starts, but definitely a mad dash. Exit at different times.*

Grandad   It wasn't always like this.

A&E Worker   I work in A&E, mostly old in the winter and drunks in the summer, working hard to keep the waiting times to a minimum, while reassuring the frightened, or in pain.

Postman   I'm a postman, out all day, keeping my eye on the lonely and old, having a chat, saying 'how are you?' as I do my rounds.

Banker   I work in a bank, people respect me, trust me. I help them sort out their money, help them get a mortgage if they can afford it.

Boss   I own and run a small firm, a family business. It's important to me that my workers are happy and secure – it makes for a better workforce, and it makes me feel better too.

Music: O'Jays – For The Love of Money: (Snatch of 'Money, Money, Money, Money').

Natalie　Biscuits. My mum loves making biscuits.

Natalie's mum　I love making biscuits (*Distributing biscuits around – also possibly some in audience.*)

Natalie　She's obsessed.

Natalie's mum　Well I wouldn't say obsessed, Natalie.

Natalie　She makes hundreds. Every day.

Grandad　When I was a lad women didn't work. My mother stayed at home and brought us up while my father worked. That was how it was and that was the only solution. People didn't get divorced and single parents were unheard of, unless you were a widow. And there were plenty of those because it was after the war. Everybody knew their place and everybody knew the system. Then I met your grandma and the world started changing. Your grandma made biscuits, she taught your mum.

Natalie's mum　Butter, flour, sugar. It's dead simple really.

Natalie　(*really stroppy*) Why can't you just buy them like everyone else?

A&E Worker　They're really tasty . . .

Postman　Lovely . . .

Dog Volunteer and Gas Worker　We love them . . .

Postman　They're lovely . . .

Banker　Ooh yes, almost as good as shop bought . . .

Postman　Better than shop bought . . .

Boss　Surprisingly good, for a hobby . . .

Natalie's mum　Hobby?

Banker　My hobby's gardening – as soon as I'm home from the office, it's straight out into the garden, Dahlias mainly.

Dog Shelter Volunteer   I love to sew in the evenings, after the children are in bed. I make all my own dresses, my husband's shirts, my children's clothes.

Gas Board Worker   I like driving, nothing better, should have been a bus driver, but I work for the gas board, weekends though we go miles.

A&E Worker   Football.

Postman   Reading.

Boss   Martial arts.

Gas Board Worker   Fishing.

Dog Shelter Volunteer   Painting.

Boss   We've all got hobbies, but we do them after work. We don't just sit around making biscuits.

Natalie's mum   (*insulted*) I work. I work every day, and nobody pays me because nobody thinks motherhood's important. I get benefits because I'm bringing up my children, looking after Grandad, keeping my eye on the neighbour's kids, helping the community – somebody's got to do it, it might as well be me.

Boss   Motherhood isn't working. Biscuits is a hobby.

Music: O'Jays – Snatch of 'Money, Money, Money, Money'.

Grandad   Of course Grandma didn't only make biscuits. She was a hippy to begin with, loved the smell of patchouli. I used to wash in it, just to get her attention. Then we had a short ceremony in a registry office, but we didn't call it marriage because we were anti patriarchal and anti establishment and your grandmother burnt her bra and was busy marching and campaigning. She wasn't alone – that would have been stupid – there were millions of them, women, marching and protesting. So, we had a 'partnership' and we both wore dungarees and we both wore patchouli and we watched Rosie the Riveter and tried to change the world.

Natalie   I can't imagine Grandma marching.

Grandad   She did, Natalie, she'd march for hours, march for miles.

Natalie   I wish I'd known her better.

Dennis' mum   My mum was the same, fighting for equality. She said anything a man can do a woman can do while holding a baby in one hand and making dinner with the other.

Dennis   What, Grandma said that?

Dennis' mum   Yes, Dennis, Grandma said that. Grandma wasn't always old.

N Friend 1   My grandma was at Greenham Common.

D Friend 1   My grandma 'reclaimed the night'.

N Friend 2   My grandma says it was all nonsense; women should be ladylike and feminine.

D Friend 2   My grandma said leave it up to the men.

N Friend 3   My grandma started her own business.

D Friend 3   My grandma shaved her head and lived on a bus.

N Friend 4   My grandma said women didn't need equality, they were better than men already.

D Friend 4   My grandma said nature dictates a difference.

N Friend 5   My grandma played football for England Ladies.

D Friend 5   My grandma was part of the peace convoy.

Grandad   My grandma said women had ways to get their own way.

Natalie's mum   (*to* **Natalie**) Your grandma campaigned for equality and choice.

Grandad   True she did.

Natalie's mum   So I'm choosing, and a stay at home mum is my choice.

D Friends 1–5   Motherhood isn't working.

N Friends 1–5   Motherhood is natural.

Natalie's mum   So I'm not allowed to be natural? I have to do something unnatural and dump my kids for a bob or two at best?

D Friends 1–5   So what did the grandads campaign for?

Grandad   The grandads campaigned to stand back and bide their time till the dust settled.

Dennis's mum   My dad worked at the car factory. Dirty, noisy, unhealthy. Everybody said they were always on strike but they weren't. I went to a grammar school; they had loads of them in those days. It was a girls' school and a few of us were working class; they had working class in those days too. But the others, the middle class girls and their parents would say, 'Your dad's on strike *again*, he's ruining this country. The unions are getting greedy, the unions have gone too far' And I would think, 'how far is too far'? And I'd notice that these girls had more than me, their parents had more than my parents. So, how far is too far? Is too far the same wage as theirs? Is too far the same road as theirs? The same clothes, the same house, the same food? They didn't want factory men to get 'above their station' and I thought, 'I'm never going to work for somebody, I'm never going to be thought of as less, as worth less, as paid less – a ceiling on my reward, a minimum for my efforts. I'm never going to be like my dad. I'm going to go as far as these girls and their parents, and then I'm going to go farther. My dad's car factory closed down, my dad was made redundant, he never worked again. They didn't want him.

D Friend 1   Blame the unions, they went too far.

D Friend 2   Blame the sixties, too permissive, not knowing your place.

N Friend 3   Blame Thatcher, destroying the unions.

D Friend 4   Blame Edward Heath joining the Common Market . . .

D Friend 5   Blame women's liberation . . .

N Friend 1   immigration . . .

N Friend 2   deregulation. . . .

D Friend 3   nationalisation . . .

N Friend 4–5   privatisation . . .

Natalie's mum   Bob Dylan.

Dennis, Natalie, D Friends 1–5, N Friends 1–5   Bob Dylan?

Music: Bob Dylan – The Times They Are A Changin'.

Grandad   And then we had your mother and slowly the patchouli got too expensive and the dungarees became inconvenient, but we still believed in equality. Your grandmother still fought and she still campaigned, but she also made biscuits and fairy cakes and told your mother stories at bedtime about how the prince was rescued by the princess and how they all lived equally ever after.

Music: Bob Dylan – The Times They Are A Changin' (Reprise).

Grandad   Natalie met Dennis over the park. They were like two ships passing in the night.

Natalie *and* **Dennis** *skateboard/scooter from either side and pass.*

Grandad   And they must have liked what they saw because. . . .

Natalie *and* **Dennis** *skateboard/scooter back from other side.*
Natalie *and* **Dennis**'s *groups appear from each side – bit of menacing circling, like* West Side Story.

Dennis   Got my new board/scooter, cost a packet. I just threw the old one in a skip, got bored with it.

D Friend 1   Cool.

D Friend 2   Wicked.

D Friend 3   Bad.

D Friend 4   Sick.

D Friend 5   Awesome.

Grandad   Very impressive.

Dennis   (*to* **Natalie**) Nice board/scooter, where'd you get it?

Natalie   Found it in a skip.

D Friend 1   Loser.

D Friend 2   (*sarcastic*) In a skip?

Natalie   I got it for free, so who's the biggest loser?

Grandad   Not a great start.

Menacing interaction between the two groups – sizing each other up, hostile. Possibly working up to a dance off or similar.

N Friend 1   *These rich kids,*

N Friend 2   *going to the posh school.*

N Friend 3   *They think they're so*

N Friend 4   *la-di-da,*

N Friend 5   *think they've got so much.*

D Friend 1   *These poor kids,*

D Friend 2   *so distrusting,*

D Friend 3   *so uptight,*

D Friend 4   *think they're so cool,*

D Friend 5   *think they're so right.*

N Friend 1–5   *Walking around with a smell under their nose.*

D Friend 1–5   *A chip on their shoulder.*

N Friend 1–5   *An air of superiority.*

D Friend 1–5   *A glare of hostility,*

N Friend 1–5   *thinking they're better,*

D Friend 1–5   *thinking they're better.*

N Friend 1–5   *Doing it with money.*

D Friend 1–5   *Doing it without.*

Dennis   My mum's the owner and CEO of a big clothing business.

Natalie   My mum's a mum.

Dennis   But what does she do?

Natalie   She's a mum.

Dennis   You mean she's unemployed?

Natalie   No, I mean she's a mum!

Natalie   (*to herself/audience*)

I'm not ashamed and I'll never say it's so,
but I'm the only one without a Nintendo.
Or an Xbox, iPhone, iPad, wii,
wide screen plasma HDTV.
And my mates go shopping and my friends buy stuff.
And I've got homemade and it's not quite good enough.
My mum grows vegetables, makes cakes and pies,
keeps chickens, knits and sews and mends and dyes.
But why can't she just buy.
For once, just one time, why can't she go out and buy!

N Friends 1–5   *These rich kids, going to the posh school. They think they're so la-di-da, think they've got so much.*

D Friends 1–5   *These poor kids, so distrusting, so uptight, think they're so cool, think they're so right.*

N Friends 1–5   *Walking around with a smell under their nose.*

D Friends 1–5   *A chip on their shoulder.*

N Friends 1–5   *An air of superiority.*

D Friends 1–5   *A glare of hostility,*

N Friends 1–5   *thinking they're better,*

D Friends 1–5   *thinking they're better.*

N Friends 1–5   *Doing it with money.*

D Friends 1–5   *Doing it without.*

Natalie   And where's your mum?

Dennis   Working.

Natalie   What, all the time?

Dennis   She's busy, she runs a business – it's important.

Natalie   More important than you?

Dennis   Well at least we're not poor.

Dennis   (*to himself/audience*)

*Working. She's always working. She starts early, she finishes
late.
'At the weekend, wait for the weekend' she says, so I wait.
But most times at the weekend she's working, she's working late.
'When you're a business woman, Dennis, it's not just nine to five,
in the early days it's work and work and work just to survive.'
In the early days it's working. In the middle years it's working.
For ever now she's working. Her hobby now is working.
Her dreams at night are working. Her life is always working.
But I'm proud. I think my mum is fabulous and I'm proud that she's
my mum.*

Natalie   (*to herself/audience at same time as* **Dennis**)

*In the early days it was stay at home mum.
In the middle years it's stay at home mum.
For ever now she's stay at home mum.
Her hobby now is stay at home mum.
Her dreams at night are stay at home mum.
Her life is always stay at home mum.
But I'm proud. I think my mum is fabulous and I'm proud that she's
my mum.*

N Friends 1–5   *These rich kids, going to the posh school. They
think they're so la-di-da, think they've got so much.*

D Friends 1–5   *These poor kids, so distrusting, so uptight, think
they're so cool, think they're so right.*

Natalie   (*to herself/audience*) I think he's cool.

Dennis   (*to himself/audience*) I think she's cool.

N Friends 1–5   *Walking around with a smell under their nose.*

D Friends 1–5   *A chip on their shoulder.*

Natalie   (*to herself*) His mum sounds important.

Dennis   (*to himself*) Her mum sounds involved.

N Friends 1–5   *An air of superiority.*

D Friends 1–5   *A glare of hostility.*

Natalie   (*to herself*) A mover and a shaker.

Dennis   (*to himself*) A homemaker and baker.

N Friends 1–5   *Thinking they're better,*

D Friends 1–5   *thinking they're better.*

Natalie   (*to herself*) I want a mum like her.

Dennis   (*to himself*) I want a mum like her.

N Friends 1–5   *Doing it with money.*

D Friends 1–5   *Doing it without.*

Natalie   (*to herself*) I think he's cool.

Dennis   (*to himself*) I think she's cool.

Grandad   Natalie and Dennis, either side of the great divide.

*Either a tussle between the two groups or an accident on **Dennis**'s scooter/skateboard, but **Dennis** gets injured. **Natalie's mum** intervenes.*

Natalie's mum   Hey, hey, hey, what's all this?

Music: Jessie J – Price Tag.

Natalie's mum   Call me old fashioned but I like kids. I like having kids, bringing up kids, looking after kids, cooking for kids, talking to kids, playing with kids. I like it when my kids bring other kids over. I like a houseful of kids. I quite often cook for my houseful of kids,

Grandad   not just biscuits but lunch, dinner

Natalie's mum   – mind you, none of the parents ever pay me. Have a biscuit, Dennis.

Dennis   These are really nice. Did you get them from an artisan bakery?

Natalie   No, she got them from the kitchen.

Natalie's mum   Butter, flour, sugar, chocolate chips. I just bash a bar with a rolling pin – seems to work and it's a lot cheaper than buying them ready bashed.

Dennis's mum   I don't have time for biscuits. I want the best for my children. I think it's important that they have a good education, which means paying obviously. That they live in a good area, which means paying obviously. That they live in a nice house.

Nanny, Au Pair, Gardener, Cleaner   Which means paying obviously.

Dennis's mum   Good teeth.

Nanny   Paying.

Dennis's mum   Good health.

Au Pair   Paying.

Dennis's mum   Varied interests.

Gardener   Paying.

Dennis's mum   Useful hobbies.

Cleaner   Paying.

+ Nanny   Paying,

+ Au Pair   paying,

+ Gardener   paying.

Dennis's mum   Sometimes I just don't know how I cope.

Nanny, Au Pair, Gardener, Cleaner   Rush, rush, rush, busy, busy, busy, business doesn't run itself.

Dennis's mum   (*to* **Natalie's mum**) I envy you really.

Dennis   Do you, Mum?

Dennis's mum   (*to* **Dennis**) Course not Dennis, they're as poor as Poundland. Biscuits? What kind of a job is biscuits?

Nanny, Au Pair   Biscuits isn't working.

Gardener, Cleaner   Biscuits isn't a job.

Music: Pulp – Common People.

Politician   Good morning.

Private Secretary and Press Aide   How do you do.

Politician   I hope I can count on your support. I hope I can count on your vote . . .

Politician, PS and PA   Hard working families.

Politician   This government supports hard working families. They are the backbone of the economy and we applaud their endeavours.

PS   We applaud their aspiration.

PA   We applaud their ability to roll up their sleeves and get on with it when times get a bit tough.

Politician   And we know that this country can go further when people work harder, when business is allowed the freedom of initiative. When worker and management work together,

PS   for the good of the country

PA   and the good of each other.

Politician   A harmonious partnership, that's what we're striving for. We can achieve greater if we all pull together. A vote for me is a vote for harmony.

Grandad   S/he means s/he wants the business class to run the show. Wants to attract big business, wants to attract the corporates, wants the country to go P L C.

Dennis's mum   I want my children to be leaders, not followers, to be at the top, not the bottom. I want them to have more than I had, does that make me a bad parent, a bad person?

Natalie's mum   But if you're working all the time you never see your kids.

Dennis's mum   I see them often enough . . . well, not 'enough' but . . . when I do it's quality time, it's not wasted time.

Natalie's mum   I just think it's important to be there for my kids, to give them a solid foundation. To show them that there's more to life than money. That's just me, I'm not judging anybody. But a lot of people judge me.

Timetable Girl   I have ballet on Monday, violin on Tuesday, piano on Wednesday, stage school Thursday, French class Friday, horse riding Saturday and swimming on Sunday. (*Whispers.*) I'd much rather read books.

Fishing Boy   I like fishing and I knew the line and tackle and stuff cost a lot for my mum and dad, so now I'm determined every time I go, which is most weekends, that I catch a nice fish for our tea, and occasionally an extra one for my nan.

Tap Shoes Mum   My daughter wanted tap shoes, wanted to do tap dancing, we scrimped and scraped and managed to get a pair second hand, just her size, then blow me down, she stopped going. Luckily, her brother took it up and not only is he obsessed but he's also the same shoe size – at the moment.

Boarding School Girl   I go to boarding school – v. exclusive. Got everything I need, and more. See my parents occasionally, they work a lot abroad, travelling, jetting around, meeting all the right people, v. important. I stay at school for most of the holidays – we try to get together at Christmas.

Disabled Son's Dad   My son's disabled but he didn't want to go to the special school, wanted to go to the ordinary school like his brothers and sister. We fought and fought and they said he couldn't but eventually we won. You do it for your kids. When nobody else cares, you just have to fight.

Maths Boy   I try really hard at maths. I'm not very good but I need a grade C at least to stay on at sixth form. My parents are paying for a maths tutor once a week and I'm trying really hard. I don't know where they get the extra money from.

Timetable Girl   Breakfast club at half past seven. After school club till half past six. Picked up by the childminder, fed by the childminder, Mum picks me up at eight, in bed by nine. They're both working really hard, overtime and extra, saving up and tightening belts, they want me to go private when I go to big school. I see my dad at weekends. My parents are not divorced.

Dennis   Sometimes doing your best for your kids doesn't involve money.

Dennis's mum   I have aspired to something better than biscuits, there is nothing wrong with that.

Dennis   But you're never home.

Dennis's mum   Because I'm doing it for you, Dennis. You have no idea what it's like to be poor, to be working class, to be ordinary. Getting told what hours to work, what money you're paid, what holidays to take. They can hire you, fire you, promote you, demote you. You have no control. You don't work for yourself, you work for them. That's what life was like for your Grandad.

Dennis   But life's not like that any more.

Dennis's mum   Oh yes it is. Don't make the mistake of thinking anything changes. In this world business leaders are the only thing that counts. Entrepreneurs are the only thing we value. I know, I've been on both sides. And I know what side I want to stay on, and I know what side I want you on.

Music: O'Jays – Snatch of 'Money, Money, Money, Money'.

Natalie   Everybody else's mum has got a job, why can't you?

Natalie's mum   Don't you like me being at home?

Natalie   I would like it better if we were like everybody else and you got a job.

Natalie's mum   I've got a job.

Natalie   No you haven't. You're just a mum.

Natalie's mum   Don't say that Natalie, that's hurtful.

Natalie   But we've never got any money and we've never got any stuff, never have nice food, or clothes that aren't second hand or Christmas presents. We can't afford to have fancy things, can't afford a holiday, can't afford to have fun and you don't seem to care.

Natalie's mum   (*to herself/audience*) Why is it all about work? When did this start? This desperate push to work all hours for such little reward? Not enough money, not enough fun. Struggling to juggle. Making ends meet. It's not about life it's not about living it's just about money. What happened? Life wasn't work obsessed when I was a kid.

Politician   Hello, pleased to meet you,

PS and PA   good morning.

Politician   Can I count on your vote? Hello little girl and what do you do?

Miranda   My name is Miranda and I am two.

Politician   But what do you do?

Miranda   I'm two.

Politician   Well what would you like to do?

Miranda   I'd like to be a princess.

Politician   (*to* **PS**) Put her down for a job in sales. Hello little boy and what would you like to be?

David   My name is David and I am three.

Politician   And what would you like to be?

David   I'm three.

Politician   But what would you like to be?

David   I'd like to be a footballer.

Politician   (*to* **PA**) Put him down for a job in sales.

Politician, **PS** *and* **PA** *exit*

Grandad   In Grandma's time men earned the money and did important things like rule the world and women cleaned the house, brought up the kids, provided the meals, looked after his majesty and seethed with resentment because they were taken for granted and were supposed to know their place. Men strutted around the world while women held it up. But then things changed . . . (*announces*) A brief history of women's liberation!

All *gather into two big groups, girls and boys. Much preparation as though for a big scene/number.*

Girls   We can do it!

Boys   No you can't!

Girls   Yes we can!

Disperse

Dennis   (*awkward, shy*) I'm sorry I called you poor.

Natalie   (*defensive/aggressive*) It's okay, we are.

Dennis   But . . .

Natalie   (*interrupts*) But my mum was there when you were hurt, your mum wasn't. And as my mum says, 'There's more to being poor than just money'.

Grandad   But then Grandma started noticing that even women didn't think that what women did was important. She started noticing that women wanted to do what men did.

Natalie's mum   Natalie's wrong, I do care. Of course I care. But being with my children is more important than over-providing for them. We all need money, I don't want them to starve, and I do my best, but I worry all the time.

Dennis's mum   I worry all the time.

Natalie's mum   I've never got enough.

Dennis's mum   You can never have enough.

Natalie   So why don't you get a job?

Natalie's mum   All right, all right. (*to herself*) Life is just about money and I've never got enough. We've never got enough.

Dennis's mum   You can never have enough.

Music: O'Jays – Money, Money, Money, Money.

Politician   Hard working families. This government cares about **you**,

PS   wants to help **you**.

PA   Help **you** get back into work if you've been away.

Politician   Or help to get you started if you've never worked before. Help if things have been difficult and your chosen career has eluded you. Yes, it's not much but you get paid in dignity and self respect. You can sleep soundly at night knowing that your contribution is greatly valued by this government.

PS   And if you work hard

PA   and work your way up

Politician   you will always be rewarded. Because we care. About **you**.

Grandad   S/he means s/he wants the less well off to work more for less. Which means the better off should employ more for less.

PS   What do you do?

PA   What's special about you?

Politician   How do you provide the glue for society?

A&E Worker   I work at the hospital, mostly nights, mostly A&E. Friday night and Saturday night it's mostly shootings and stabbings. I don't know what the world's coming to.

Postman   I'm a postman, used to love it till they started telling us how fast we had to walk. I can walk it, sometimes faster, but I just resent them taking the joy out of the job.

Banker   I had a job, in a bank, not like those bankers they have now. People keep saying 'Oh, you're one of those banker types are you?' But I'm not. Anyway I got made redundant, probably because they couldn't afford to pay all those banker types' bonuses.

Boss   My business has grown and grown. My workforce is in the thousands and I have branches up and down the country. We're thinking of expanding into Europe.

Dog Shelter Volunteer   I wanted to be a vet but I couldn't do the maths, so now I volunteer at the dog shelter. I'm not working at the moment, I have no time to be employed, there are too many strays.

PS   You have to get a job.

Natalie's Mum   I've got a job.

PA   What job?

Natalie's Mum   Looking after my kids job.

Appropriate Chorus   Being a mum job.

PS   That's not a job.

Natalie's Mum   Yes it is.

PA   It's not on my list of 'what the government accepts as jobs'.

Natalie's Mum   I don't care.

Appropriate Chorus   We don't care.

PS   Not on my list of 'What will bring the unemployment statistics down'.

Natalie's Mum   I don't care.

Appropriate Chorus   We don't care.

PA   Not on my list of 'What will help the government get re-elected'.

Appropriate Chorus + Grandad + N Mum + D Mum   We don't care.

Politician   (*menacing*) You have to get a job.

Grandad   In Grandma's day women's work wasn't taken seriously. Nobody thought it was important, nobody thought it was worth doing, and certainly not worth paying. That was fifty–odd years ago. Nothing's changed.

Natalie   (*calling over*) Dennis? Want to come to our house for dinner?

Dennis   Yes okay . . . . please.

D Friend 3   I'm getting a takeaway anyone want to share?

N Friend 3   I will.

N Friend 4   I'm stuck on history homework.

D Friend 4   I love history.

N Friend 5   How do people get to work on the stock market?

D Friend 5   My dad works on the stock market.

Music: Pulp – Common People (Reprise).

Politician   Zero unemployment is a vote winner. The people need to see that I'm steering a tight ship. So, get the newspapers involved, we want articles about benefit scroungers, people who refuse to work.

PS   People who take millions from the welfare budget.

PA   And contribute nothing.

PS   Who sit around all day with booze and fags and let their kids run wild.

PA   Getting into crime, into gangs

PS   young thugs menacing the community

PA   terrifying the state.

Politician   You know the sort of thing.

PS   We'll get TV involved – gritty reality.

PA   Life on an estate.

PS   The drugs, the drink, the violence.

PA   The stabbings, the shootings, the gangland overlords.

PS   Unemployed living next to decent people,

PA   bringing down the neighbourhood.

PS   Bringing down the house prices.

PA   Hard working families struggling to survive amongst feckless, lazy, scroungers living on welfare, living off the state.

Politician   The sort of thing that will get me re-elected.

Placard 1   Day One. Four Million Unemployed

PA   (*to random 'people in the street'*) Excuse me what do you think about unemployed people?

Adult Chorus   (1) Well there's probably a good reason. (2) It's not easy to get a job in this day and age. (3)Too many government cuts.

Placard 2   Day Two. Britain Isn't Working

Adult Chorus   (1) No more factories. (2) No more manufacturing. (3) No steel works. (4) Not much of a car industry. (5) No Mining. (6) No shipyards.

Placard 2   Day Three. Get On Your Bike

Adult Chorus   (1) They should perhaps widen their search. (2) There are jobs, people just have to look for them. (3) Travel further. (4) They should get on their bikes.

Placard 4   Day Four. Benefit Cheats

Adult Chorus   (1) There's plenty of jobs, they're just not trying. (2) Some people aren't prepared to look. (3) Aren't prepared to travel. (4) Aren't prepared to work.

Placard 5   Day Five. Single Mum Gets a million in Housing Benefit

Adult Chorus   (1) They want it easy. (2) Want jobs to just fall into their laps. (3) Won't do the dirty work. (4) Want someone else to do it.

Placard 6   Day Six. Benefit Cuts Incentive to Work

Adult Chorus   (1) They're too lazy. (2) Want to get paid to do nothing. (3) Think the world owes them a living. (4) Skivers. (5) Scroungers. (6) Scum.

Cute Kid with Placard 7   Day Seven. Who Will Win X Factor?

Politician   We all take a rest on a Sunday. It's good for the country. A diversion you might say.

Grandad   Grandma thought the majority of both men and women should only work four hours a day, that way they could share the housework and childcare, have their own income, be independent and married and parents, should they choose, have dignity and reach their own potential. Mind you by then Grandma was an anarchist. . . .

Politician, PS, PA   You have to get a job.

A&E Worker   I work at the hospital, mostly nights, mostly A&E, but I also do some days because we're stretched to the limit. There are not enough nurses and resources are tight. My pay's been frozen and patient numbers are growing because other A&Es have shut down. I don't know if I can carry on much longer.

Placard 5   Minimum wage.

Chorus   Or less.

Placard 4   Zero hours contract.

Chorus   Seasonal.

Placard 3   Part time.

Chorus   Hardly pays the bus fare.

Placard 2   There are no jobs.

Chorus   None that I can do.

Placard 1   I've got kids.

Politician, PS, PA   You have to get a job.

Postman   I'm a postman, I do bigger routes than I used to, they've squeezed a two man job into one man. Sometimes I really worry that I'm not going to get round on time. I feel like I've failed because I'm posting mail in the middle of the afternoon. Sometimes I really hate my job.

Placard 1   How am I supposed to get there?

Placard 2   What do I do with the baby?

Placard 3   What do I do with the kids?

Politician, PS, PA   Child care.

Placard 1   Child care costs a fortune.

Placard 2   More than I can earn.

Placard 3   What if one of the kids is ill?

Politician, PS, PA   You have to get a job.

Banker   I used to work in a bank, then I set myself up as a self-employed accountant. It's a struggle and I have to work all hours, take all work. I can't afford to be choosy, (*whispers*) and sometimes I'm not sure I'm legal. I make just enough to get by at the moment. Obviously I hope things will improve.

Placard 3   Why can't I just bring up my kids?

Politician   It doesn't work that way.

PS   That's not working.

PA   Motherhood isn't work.

Politician   Parenthood isn't work.

PS   Motherhood doesn't pay.

PA   Motherhood doesn't count.

Politician, PS, PA   Get a job or we'll cut your benefits.

Dog Shelter Volunteer   I stopped volunteering at the dog shelter because they said I wasn't actively seeking work and they stopped my benefits. I'm a dog walker now. People haven't time to walk their own dogs anymore. People in the park hate me because we go round like a pack, but what else can I do? I can't walk one or two at a time, it would take all day to get through them all. And some parks have banned us altogether.

Politician   Anything will do.

PS   Start at the bottom.

PA   Work your way up.

Placard 4   But I'm working already.

Politician   Put it this way

PS   if you don't

PA   you won't

Politician, PS, PA   be supported.

Placard 5   I'm on forty hours a week minimum wage.

Politician   Skiver.

PS   Scrounger.

PA   Slacker.

Chorus   It's only part time but I've got three kids under five.

Chorus   Lazing around all day watching daytime telly.

Chorus   Curtains closed mid morning.

Chorus   I'm disabled.

Chorus   Dossing.

Chorus   Living off the state.

Politician   Get a job you lazy slob.

+ PS   Get a job you lazy slob.

+ PA   Get a job you lazy slob.

PS   We pay you to give your kids to someone else, whose job it is to look after those kids while you go and work for less than what you're giving in child care.

Politician, PS, PA   So Get A Job!

Music: Queen/David Bowie – Under Pressure.

Natalie   Where are you Mum? Are you home? You must be home,

Grandad   you're always home . . .

Natalie   Mum? Mum? Where are you?

Natalie's mum   (*in frozen panic*) *I haven't got a thing to wear.*

Natalie   *It was weird. I thought she wasn't there.*

Natalie's mum   I can say it's political, I can say it's my choice to stay at home,

Grandad   and it is . . .

Natalie's mum   but . . .

Natalie   *I thought she wasn't home. I panicked, felt alone. It felt odd. I don't think I want her to get a job.*

Natalie's mum   I used to work. When I was young, before kids, I had lots of jobs. Didn't know what I wanted to do, didn't know what I wanted to be but I was happy to work, tried all sorts.

Natalie   I don't really mean it, I love her being here, I love her being my mum. It's just sometimes . . . I want to be the same as everybody else. *I thought she wasn't home. I panicked, felt alone.*

Grandad   It felt odd.

Natalie   I don't think I want her to get a job.

Natalie's mum   *I'm out of my comfort zone, I'm out of the place called me. I hide behind my kids, I'm confident with kids, but I'm scared of society. I'm out of my comfort zone, I'm not sure I look the part. I can look after kids, but kids isn't work and I don't know how to start. I haven't got a thing to wear.*

Natalie   (*to* **Dennis**) Is it like this for you?

Dennis   I can spend hours forgetting where I am, forgetting I'm alone. It doesn't bother me, I'm used to it. I like being alone. I play with my friends most days.

D Friend 1   Go to the park, hang around.

Dennis   Go back to my house and play Xbox or something.

D Friend 2   Eat toast or crisps.

Dennis   My mum says,

D Friend 3   'Who ate all the crisps, what happened to the bread?'

Dennis   I say it was me, I don't mention my friends.

D Friend 4   Don't know if she'd like us coming back,

Dennis   so I just say it was me.

D Friend 5   She doesn't really mind,

Dennis   just thinks I'm growing.

Chorus Mum 1   The kids say they don't mind coming back to an empty house but I don't like it. I worry. Anything could happen and they're not old enough to cope.

Chorus Mum 2   I'm thinking childminder, later on, when I get organised, when I see how I'm fixed. They're expensive I know, but what can I do, don't want to lose my job running home every five minutes.

Chorus Mum 3   I'm responsible if anything happens, and so many things could, they're not that old, not really old enough to look after themselves.

Chorus Mum 4   My mum lives right across town and she's got a hip, it wouldn't be right to ask her. They're good kids, sensible, they say they're all right, but I worry. Perhaps I should move nearer my mum – but that would be a hell of a journey to work.

Dennis   I eat packet pasta or noodles.

D Friend 1   I like that.

Dennis   Sometimes I'll stick a jacket potato in the oven, but it takes forever.

D Friend 2   And I get bored waiting.

D Friend 3   Crisps,

D Friend 4   biscuits,

D Friend 5   convenience food . . .

Dennis   Sometimes I just eat cereal, but I don't tell her if she asks.

D Friend 1   They'll leave money for pizza or Chinese or whatever, but I'm not keen on pizza and to be honest, I don't like opening the door, so I keep it and spend it later,

D Friend 2–5   sweets or whatever.

Dennis   Sometimes I go to bed alone.

Natalie's mum   *I haven't got a thing to wear.*

Natalie   *You must have something. Just iron a few things, comb your hair.*

Dennis and D Friends 1–5   *Crisps, biscuits, convenience food.*

Natalie's mum   When was the last time I bought anything for me?

Natalie   What about Primark? Can't you borrow from somebody?

Natalie's mum   *I haven't got a thing to wear.*

Dennis and D Friends 1–5   *Jacket potato if I'm in the mood.*

Natalie   When you've got a job you can buy something smart.

Natalie's mum   Until I've got a job I can't afford to.

Dennis and D Friends 1–5   *Crisps, biscuits, convenience food. Jacket potato if I'm in the mood.*

Natalie's mum   I *haven't got a thing to wear*. I look such a scruff. I've had this top for years. Look at my shoes. I can't go to an interview in these shoes. I can't look for a job with my hair like this. I haven't got any makeup haven't worn it for years. I used to look good, I used to look fab but now . . . (*Looking at herself.*) who'd employ this?

Grandad   I would.

Natalie's mum   But I look such a scruff. I haven't got a thing to wear . . . Let's hit the charity shops.

Natalie   Charity shops?

Natalie's mum   Yes. Cheap, cheerful . . . and sometimes you can pick up a real bargain.

(**Natalie's mum** *getting changed during the next bit, repeat till ready.*)

Natalie   *Let's hit the charity shops.*

Natalie's mum   *What would we do without charity shops.*

Grandad   *Looks like new in charity shops.*

Dennis's mum   *Give something too to charity shops.*

N Friend 1   *We're going to hit the charity shops.*

N Friend 2   *Can't get through without charity shops.*

N Friend 3   *Looks like new in charity shops.*

Dennis's mum   *Give something too to charity shops.*

N Friend 4   *You need some shoes from charity shops.*

N Friend 5   *Some shoes you can choose from charity shops.*

Natalie   *I want a dress from a charity shop.*

Natalie's mum   *I look such a mess need a charity shop.*

All Girls   *Need a skirt, need a blouse, need a jacket, need some shoes.*

All Boys   *Need a shirt need a tie need a jacket need some shoes.*

All   *Something nice, something sharp, something stylish, something dark. Something suitable, commutable, work wise irrefutable. Look the part, office smart, office best, stay-pressed.*

Grandad   *Clothes for interviews.*

Dennis's mum   *Clothes that look like new.*

Natalie's mum   (*to* **Dennis's mum**) *Clothes that say I look like you.*

Natalie's mum *and* **Dennis's mum** *dressed the same – career women.*

Music: Michael Jackson – Man in the Mirror.

Grandad   Grandma started fighting the system. She wasn't a communist though, she thought that system was wrong too. Anything that was big government or big corporations and conglomerates were faceless and therefore soulless according to Grandma. She wanted more local, organic, artisan, small businesses rather than big. She even believed in bartering. There was space for it in those days. Alternatives. She said there had to be a male principle and a female principle, there had to be balance.

Natalie   This is my world . . .

(**Natalie**'s *house/world shabby and full of people and noise – the stage bright, loud, pop music, people working together loud and chaotic and squashed.* **Dennis** *and his group joining in slightly, feeling what it's like.*)

Dennis   And this is my world . . .

(**Dennis**'s *house/world very up to the minute and ordered and quiet. The* **nanny**, **au pair**, **gardener**, **cleaner** *going about their business efficiently. People reading or working quietly. The stage sombre, subdued, classical music, working quietly, plenty of space.* **Natalie** *and her group joining in slightly, feeling what it's like.*)

Natalie   I love your house.

N Friend 1   It's so full of stuff.

N Friend 2   Gadgets.

N Friend 3   State of the art TV.

N Friend 4   All the games consoles.

N Friend 5   Really cool furniture and your fridge is *stocked!*

Dennis   I love your house. It's friendly. It's fun. More together, cosier. And your mum's there. Whenever you need her . . .

Natalie   But. . . .

Dennis   But?

Natalie   But we're poor. My mum's not working. Biscuits isn't working.

Music: UB40 – One in Ten.

Postman *gives P45 to* **A&E Worker**, **Dog Shelter Volunteer**, **Gas Board Worker**, **Tap Shoes Mum**, **Disabled Son's Dad**, **Placard 2**, **Banker**, **Placard 4**, **Placard 5**. *They then join the dole queue. Then* **Politician** *gives P45 to* **Postman**.

Politician   Everyone can succeed if they work hard. This government rewards hard working people, hard working families.

PS   We create opportunity,

PA   Aspiration.

Grandad   Of course it also helps if you've been privately educated, have above average intelligence or know the right people. And trampling on people and society to get to the top doesn't hurt either.

Politician   We are cutting the rates of unemployment. Streamlining the welfare state. We will have

PS   a better,

PA   brighter

Politician, PS, PA   Britain.

A&E Worker   *Let's go down the job centre,*

Postman   *I want a job from the job centre,*

Dog Shelter Volunteer   *need to earn a bob at the job centre,*

Gas Board Worker   *you get a mob at my job centre.*

Tap Shoes Mum   *I want a job that's new.*

Disabled Son's Dad   *I don't know what I can do.*

Placard 2   *Want to be a doctor, want to be a nurse,*

Banker   *want to be a burglar or something slightly worse.*

Placard 4   *Want a job that pays a lot,*

Placard 5   *want a job with Microsoft,*

All Above   *I want to be rich, I want to be rich, I want to be rich, I want to be rich.*

A&E Worker   I could have done factories, shipyards, mining, steel.

Postman   But they're gone now, all those jobs have gone.

Dog Shelter Volunteer   I'm not the brightest, I'm a little bit thick, but I still want more than a zero hours contract.

Gas Board Worker   Minimum wage, no security McJob.

Tap Shoes Mum   I just want the opportunity to work.

Disabled Son's Dad   I just want the advantage of a decent pay packet.

Placard 2   My old job is now done by computer.

Banker   My old job is now done by robots.

Placard 4   Mine's been relocated up North.

Placard 5   To India.

All Above   To China.

Music: UB40 – One In Ten (Reprise).

Job Centre Worker   What are you good at? What can you do?

PS   What do you do?

PA   What's special about you?

Politician   How do you provide the glue for society?

Natalie's mum   I haven't worked for years, I don't know what to do. Everybody has moved forward, advanced, danced with computers and what is text? How do I twitter? What is a water cooler moment? People will talk about all this stuff that I don't know anything about. (*to* **JCW**) I'm good with kids, I can do something with kids.

Job Centre Worker   (*fast and bored*) Nanny, childminder, baby sitter, au pair, teaching assistant, teacher, ESL teacher, special needs teacher, primary school teacher, secondary school teacher, sixth form college teacher, after school assistant, paediatric nurse, social worker, youth club worker, childcare worker, charity worker, dinner lady, nursery nurse, sweet shop assistant, GCSE maths.

Natalie's mum   What?

Job Centre Worker   GCSE maths?

Natalie's mum   Oh. No.

Job Centre Worker   Lollipop lady. But there's no vacancies. Cleaner. All the best houses want a cleaner. Loads of people want cleaners nowadays, because they're too busy working to clean their own house. You could be a cleaner or go back to school.

Natalie's mum   Cleaner? But I got all dressed up. Aren't there any other jobs? There must be something else. Must be something I can do?

JCW *shrugs*

Music: Robbie Williams – Let Me Entertain You.

Music blaring. Big set up like a game show studio, **Chorus** *playing audience, who loudly reply 'Get A Job!' and cheer every time Get A Job gets uttered*

Game show host   Let's play, Get A Job! Good evening ladies and gentlemen and welcome to Get A Job! The weekly game show where one lucky contestant gets set up for life and nobody leaves empty handed. So without further ado let's meet the contestants on Get A Job!

Lovely Assistant 1   Tell us about yourself Contestant One.

Contestant One   I'm just an ordinary sort of chap – prep school, private school, boarding school . . .

Game show host   Isn't your father Lord Poshity Poshity Posh Posh?

Contestant One   Oh yes absolutely . . . But I want to be prime minister in twenty years time so I need an ordinary sort of job for a few months to show I'm 'one of the people' when I go into politics. I don't just want to take over Poshity Hall and be called remote and out of touch with the electorate.

Game show host   Marvellous, marvellous. Well we wish you all the best and good luck on Get A Job!

Lovely Assistant 2   Contestant Two, tell us a little about why you're here on Get A Job!

Contestant Two   I got a 2.1 at Uni okay? And I've sent in like five hundred and twenty-six job applications? And I still haven't got a job? And all my friends said like 'up your profile?' so, here I am?

Game show host   So you're hoping to win big tonight?

Contestant Two   Well, like yeah?

Game show host   Okay good, well we wish you all the luck, I really mean that. (*To 'audience'.*) Yes? Yes!

Lovely Assistant 3   Contestant Three, tell us a little about yourself.

Natalie's mum   Um . . . I'm just a housewife and mother who needs to get a job . . .

'Audience' yell Get A Job! to **Natalie's mum's** *surprise*

Game show host   Just a housewife and mother, do you hear that ladies and gentlemen? Just a housewife and mother, how quaint. Isn't that marvellous everybody? You see we try to bring a little bit of nostalgia into every show, every edition of Get A Job! Marvellous, wonderful, we wish you all the luck in the world, I mean that most sincerely, I really do . . . . (*To 'audience'.*) okay who wants to play Get A Job?! As you can see ladies and gentlemen this is all fair, we operate on a level playing field and it's entirely due to the contestants' abilities and talents whether they succeed or not.

Lovely Assistant 1   We have no gender bias,

Lovely Assistant 2   no race bias,

Lovely Assistant 3   no class bias.

Game show host   Contestants win on their own merits. Okay let's get started. It's time to play Get A Job!!!!! Now think carefully, try to answer correctly, we want one of you to win, we really do . . . . Okay (*Reading from question cards.*) Have you been privately educated?

Move forward **Contestant One**

Game show host   Do you have A levels?

Move forward **Contestant One** *and* **Two**.

Game show host   Have you been to university?

Move forward **Contestant One** *and* **Two**.

Game show host   Have you been to Oxbridge?

Move forward **Contestant One**.

Game show host   And for a possible win. . . . Do you, or your parents know the boss?

Contestant One *wins.*

Game show host   Well done! Well done! Good game, good game. Didn't he do well? You've just won a job with the establishment – have a load of money!

Lovely Assistant 1, *showers* **Contestant One** *with money, possibly wheeled on in a wheelbarrow.*

Game show host   Okay, okay, calm down, calm down, let's contain the excitement ladies and gentlemen . . . (*To contestants.*) You're still in it. Everything to play for. 2nd prize, not to be sneezed at. . . . For the runner up prize: (*Reading from card again.*) Can you work nights?

Move forward **Contestant Two**.

Game show host   Can you work weekends?

Move forward **Contestant Two**.

Game show host   Can you work before the kids go to school?

Move forward **Contestant Two**.

Game show host   Can you work after the kids have come home from school?

Move forward **Contestant Two**.

Game show host   Did you understand anything the maths teacher ever taught you?

Contestant Two *and* **Natalie's mum** *hesitate, look at each other, almost move forward, then shake their heads, no.*

Game show host   Have you got at least a few GCSEs?

Move forward **Contestant Two** *and* **Natalie's mum**, *who punches the air with excitement.*

Game show host   And, possibly for the round . . . Do you or your parents know the boss?

Contestant Two *wins.*

Game show host   Well done! You've just won an average job with an average wage – you can afford to go abroad this summer – have a packet of biscuits for those water cooler moments!

Lovely Assistant 2 *presents a packet of hobnobs with much fanfare and scene stealing.*

Game show host   Now then our lovely mum.

Lovely Assistants 1–3   Ahh.

Chorus/audience   Ahhh.

Game show host   Never mind, the questions just weren't going your way. But you don't go away empty handed, oh no, nobody leaves empty handed on this show. If you can jump through these hoops . . . You win any old job, doing the things nobody else wants to do for a minimum wage or zero hours contract.

Lovely Assistants 1–3 *each hold out a hoop, making things as difficult/humiliating/laughable or stupid as possible,* **Natalie's mum** *manages though to go through them.*

Game show host   Well done, well done, you win a nylon overall!!!!

Chorus   Yaay!

Game show host   (*aside*) You have to pay for that by the way.

Job Centre Worker   So cleaner is it? (*Helps* **Natalie's mum** *on with her overall.*)

Music: Robbie Williams – Let Me Entertain You (*Reprise*).

Interval

Act Two

Music: Madonna – Material Girl.

Natalie's mum *cleaning around, unacknowledged by* **Vicki**, **Veriti** *and* **Violette** *except when they directly speak to her.*

Vicki, Veriti and Violette   An island! We've got to have an island! (*To* **Natalie's mum**.) You've missed a bit.

Vicki   Tom?

Veriti   Dick?

Violette   Harry?

Tom, Dick and Harry   What?

Vicki   Can you work an extra shift?

Veriti   Overtime?

Violette   Take another case?

Tom, Dick and Harry   Why?

Vicki, Veriti and Violette   We've got to have an island.

Tom   In the Caribbean?

Dick   In the Canaries?

Harry   In the Galapagos?

Tom/Dick   Galapagos?

Vicki, Veriti and Violette   In the kitchen! (*To* **Natalie's mum**.) You've missed a bit.

Vicki   An island.

Veriti   A kitchen island.

Violette   Simply everyone who's anyone has got one.

Vicki, Veriti and Violette   We've got to have one.

Tom   What happened to the granite worktops?

Vicki, Veriti and Violette   So last year.

Dick   The Cotswold stone floors?

Vicki, Veriti and Violette   Yawn nostalgia.

Harry   The stainless steel surrounds, the under-floor heating, American fridge, wet rooms, decking, his and her basins, the Belfast sink, funky fuchsia finishes.

Tom/Dick/Harry   Carpets!

Natalie's mum   I remember carpets.

Vicki, Veriti and Violette   So last century.

Phones ring. **Vicki**, **Veriti** *and* **Violette** *get out their phones and listen.*

Vicki, Veriti and Violette   (*scream*) Taupe! Everything's got to be taupe!

Running exit. Then **Vicki** *dashes back.*

Vicki   (*to* **Natalie's mum**) You've missed a bit.

Exit laughing.

Natalie's mum   When I've counted up the cost of the bus fare/ train fare/ petrol, the overalls/smart clothes/equipment, sandwiches/lunches/coffees/teas, childcare/hair care/shoe wear – it comes to a pound. It comes to a pittance. A pound better off. It's hardly worth the bother. I think I'm losing money. I think I'm actually poorer. Got to get a better job. Got to work full time. Get more qualifications. Got to study.

Music: O Jay's – Money, Money, Money, Money.

Natalie's mum   I'm exhausted, the job's so. . . .

Grandad   unrewarding?

Natalie   (*hopeful*) Are you going to quit?

Natalie's mum   No, Natalie, I'm going to find something full time. I'm more in debt now I'm working than I was when I wasn't. And the benefits system . . . don't get me started! Let's make some biscuits, while we've got the time. It won't take long and it will cheer us both up.

Music: Oasis – Roll with it.

Job centre worker   Maths. English. Science. Qualifications. Exams. GCSEs. A levels. Degrees. Work experience, apprenticeship, internship. Part time, full time, seasonal, permanent.

Grandad   Then Grandma started getting involved with marches and demonstrations against capitalism. The poll tax riots, stop the city, G8, anti Monsanto. Kept getting arrested. She said never trust a politician – They're either in it for themselves or kowtowing to the party.

Politician   (*addressing crowd*) Aspiration. We can go further. Hard work will be rewarded. If you're prepared to roll up your sleeves and show initiative then you will succeed. Sell yourself. Buy aspiration and sell yourself.

PS   Buy yourself an education.

PA   And sell yourself for work.

Politician   Look at these people. (**VV&V** & **TD&H** *doing nothing.*) They work hard, they're hard working families, they've strived to get to the top.

Grandad   They started at the top.

Veriti   I've got a dishwasher.

Harry   My dad's a duke. (*To* **Tom**.) Wasn't your father a lord? (*To* **Dick**.) And wasn't your father some kind of . . . gentleman crook?

Vicki   *Mobile phones and laptops,*

Veriti   *vacuums and cars.*

Violette   *Gadgets and gizmos,*

VV&V   *smelly stuff in jars.*

Tom   *We've got rooms. Rooms and rooms and rooms.*

Dick   *Rooms above, rooms below.*

Harry   *Rooms to think, rooms to grow.*

VV&V   *Mobile phones and laptops, vacuums and cars. Gadgets and gizmos, smelly stuff in jars.*

TD&H   (*same time as* **VV&V**) *Rooms and rooms and rooms. Rooms above, rooms below. Rooms to think, rooms to grow.*

Miranda   But where's my mum?

David   I can't find my dad.

All   Where is everyone?

Grandad   Must be in another room.

Politician   Hard working families. This government rewards hard working families.

PS   If you haven't got enough,

PA   You haven't worked enough.

Grandad   And the more you've got, the more you'll spend, to show everybody how much more you've got. And how much better you are.

Miranda   Watch me Mummy . . .

David   Watch me Daddy. . . .

Miranda   Mummy?

David   Daddy?

All adults   In a minute darling, I've just got to finish work.

All chorus join in, parents and kids. Separate kids. Separate parents. Then both together.

Kids Chorus
- *Watch me Mummy.*
- *Watch me Daddy.*
- *Look at me.*
- *See what I'm doing.*
- *Look I'm doing this.*

Parents chorus
- *Not now darling.*
- *In a minute.*
- *Just give me two secs.*
- *Can't it wait till later?*
- *Can it wait till morning?*

Kids/parents chorus   *Busy, busy, busy, got to finish work.*

Building and then including **Dennis's mum** *and* **Dennis** *and various chorus types like them*

Dennis and D Friends 1–5   *Mum are you busy? Mum can you talk?*

Dennis's mum   *It's all going wrong.*

Nanny   *The market's crashing.*

Au Pair   *Stocks dropping.*

Gardener   *Confidence waning.*

Cleaner   *Got to re-brand.*

Dennis's mum   *Got to downsize.*

All together building from a whispered inward panic to a cacophony of stress. Then quiet for **Cute Kid** *to step forward.*

Cute Kid   Why do you have to work so much, Daddy? Why are you always busy, Mummy?

Chorus Daddy   (*unsure*) Because . . . we . . . need . . .

Chorus Mummy   (*also unsure*) Stuff?

Chorus Daddy   Yes stuff. We need . . .

Chorus Mummy   Stuff. We need stuff.

Chorus Daddy   Yes we do.

Chorus Mummy   We need it.

Cute Kid   Stuff?

All   Stuff!

Music: Queen/David Bowie – Under Pressure.

Chorus 1   Adverts. Buy this, buy that, buy the other.

Chorus 2   You don't need it but you want it.

Chorus 3   You've never heard of it but you have to have it.

Chorus 4   It's useless but it's necessary.

Chorus 5   Simply anyone who's anyone has got one.

Violette *watches the adverts as though watching on TV while her child stands next to her waiting to get her attention.*

Violette   (*depressed*) Worked like a dog. Saved up . . .

Vi's Child   Mum?

Violette   . . . built the extension, huge kitchen sky lights and ceiling lights, natural stone floor . . .

Vi's Child   Mum?

Advert One: (*video optional*) **'harassed housewives'** (*or just one*) *mopping the floor and their brows.*

Actor   Don't use that old mop, it simply spreads the germs further.

White lab coat scientist   It's been clinically proven that germs gather on kitchen floors, making food preparation hazardous.

Actor   Do you want this to happen to your son?

Maths Boy *walking in mopped area and 'dying' dramatically. Harassed housewives reacting accordingly.*

Actor   Or this to happen to your daughter?

Boarding School Girl *walking in mopped area and 'dying' dramatically. Harassed housewives reacting accordingly.*

White lab coat scientist   It could happen because of the way **you** clean your floor.

Actor   So throw away your old mop and use the new steams as it cleans as it disinfects, protects, sterilises, neutralises, vapourises, moisturises, gleaming, steaming, sun soaked beach and dreaming, anti bacterial mop. You owe it to your family because . . .

White lab coat scientist   it's been scientifically proven . . .

Everybody in advert   (*toothy smiles*) it kills germs not kids!

Violette   . . . .slate worktops, real oak cupboards, big fridge, ice dispenser . . .

Vi's Child   (*more insistent*) Mum?

Advert Two: (*video optional*) **Girl 1** *walking normally, minding her own business* (*again could be a whole bunch doing the same thing*).

Boy/s   (*yells*) Oi! Wrinkly! Slap some cream on!

Girl 1 *stands mortified, holding her face in alarm, as* **Girl 2** *runs up and announces to audience.*

Girl 2 (*lovingly stroking the bottle/jar*) Anti wrinkle, youth rejuvenating face crème.

Girl 1 *uses some on her face, instantly feels in heaven. She and* **Girl 2** *put their heads together, faces forward* (*cheesy cute and smiling*).

Girls   It's almost like ironing your face.

Violette   . . . dishwasher, magimix, coffee maker, Aga *and* gas range . . .

Vi's Child   (*more insistent*) Mum?

Advert Three. Chorus *couple dance like* **Fred** & **Ginger** *while each holding a can of Aspirite. A* **singer** *to the music of 'Row Row Row Right up the River' sings:*

You've got to buy, buy, buy till you feel better
You must buy buy buy like a jet setter
You must buy something good
Like you know that you should
You get in debt and get in debt
And buy to lift your mood
And then you buy buy buy a little harder
You must buy buy buy (stock up your larder)
You get everything new
but still you feel blue
and so you buy buy buy

On the last line **Fred** *and* **Ginger** *finish facing each other in a champagne arm cross to drink their Aspirite, then turn to audience.*

Fred and Ginger   Aspirite! The drink that gives you a thirst for more!

Violette   . . . all the gadgets, all the gizmos. State of the art kitchen – Why am I so miserable? What more could I want?

Vi's Child   Mum, I'm hungry.

Violette   Throw something in the microwave darling, I'm watching Jamie.

Job Centre Worker   So you need more qualifications, more GCSEs. And you have to train to get a better job.

Natalie's mum   But how can I train and also get more qualifications? Can I just quit this job in order to train?

Job Centre Worker   Leave work voluntarily and your benefits will be cut.

Natalie's mum   But how can I work and train and study? Do you help with that? Where will I find the time?

Job Centre Worker   Are you refusing employment?

Natalie's mum   No, I'm asking how I can train and study and work?

Job Centre Worker   Are you refusing the means of employment?

Natalie's mum   No, I'm asking when I'm supposed to find the time?

Job Centre Worker   Because I can cut your benefits if you refuse to work.

Natalie's mum   I'm not refusing. Okay? I'm training. I'm working. I'm studying.

Natalie (*offstage*)   Biscuits mum?

Natalie's mum   Busy, Natalie, busy.

D Friend 1   Maths: how to add up the cost of everything, multiply by the global markets, divide by social services and arrive at the value of nothing.

D Friend 2   English: how to speak at an interview, how to complete a c.v. how to spell 'employment', 'entrepreneur', 'winner', 'loser', how to talk to a customer, how to talk to a boss, how to talk to a telephone, how to talk to a machine, 'how to press 1 now'.

D Friend 3   History: learn about famous entrepreneurs, learn about successful people in past careers, learn about who earned how much for what job which in nowadays money is a hell of a lot. Learn why all wars are about economics.

D Friend 4   Geography: learn where the gold comes from, where's the oil, where's the gas, where are the mineral deposits. Which country exploits which people, who's fighting for what wealth where.

D Friend 5   Foreign languages: how to say 'work' in French, Spanish, German, Chinese, Russian.

D Friend 1   Education: How to pass exams.

D Friend 2   How to learn enough to get a job.

D Friend 3   A GCSE in jobs.

D Friend 4   An A level in work.

D Friend 5   A degree in employment.

Job Centre Worker   Everything has a price. Everything is economic, everything must compete in the global market. Everything can be bought, everyone can be sold. Life is money and money is life.

Music: O'Jays – Money, Money, Money, Money.

Job Centre Worker   In the global market everyone competes. I'm not sure who wins, or if anyone wins, but everyone competes.

Natalie's mum   I don't want this. I don't want this.

D Friends 1–5   There is no alternative.

Job Centre Worker   This is what we all do, this is how it is.

Natalie's mum   So now I'm a full time mum, with kids, and Grandad and a single parent and a housewife and a cleaner and a job seeker and a student. Where's my maths book?

Natalie (*offstage*)   Got any biscuits mum?

Natalie's mum   (*getting v. shirty*) No, Natalie, I haven't had time to make any.

Natalie (*offstage*)   Can we buy some?

Natalie's mum   No!

Grandad   Money's tight!

Music: Kaiser Chiefs – Angry Mob (end bit).

A&E   You have to get a job.

Postman   Minimum wage.

Dog Shelter Volunteer   Or less.

Gas Board Worker   Just been made redundant.

Tap Shoes Mum   The company goes up,

Disabled Son's Dad   makes no difference to you.

Placard 2   Part time doesn't pay the rent.

Banker   Hardly pays the bus fare.

Placard 4   Get a job you lazy slob.

Placard 5   The company goes down.

Union Rep   You're out on your ear.

Boss   Closing down sale.

A&E, Postman, Dog Shelter Volunteer   I've got kids.

Gas Board Worker, Tap Shoes Mum, Disabled Son's Dad   There are no jobs.

Placard 2, Banker, Placard 4   Chip away at workers' rights.

Placard 5, Union Rep, Boss   Business just went bust.

Boss   Everything must go.

A&E, Postman, Dog Shelter Volunteer   You have to get a job.

+ Gas Board, Tap Shoes Mum, Disabled Son's Dad   Give you less and work you more.

+ Placard 2, Banker, Placard 4   I worked the same job for twenty five years.

+ Placard 5, Union Rep, Boss   Living off the state.

Boss   Bankrupt.

All Above + Nanny, Au Pair, Gardener, Cleaner   Get a job you lazy slob. Zero hours contract. Chip away at the unions, Why am I not working?

Natalie's mum   Motherhood is work.

Music: Robbie Williams – Let Me Entertain You (Reprise).

Game Show Host   Good evening ladies and gentlemen and welcome to Get A Job.

Lovely Assistants 1–3   Where Are They Now?!

Chorus   (*repeat*) Get a job where are they now! Yaay!!

Game show host   I wonder if you remember this guy, Unlucky Brian? I think some of our more dedicated viewers may think he looks familiar. So familiar in fact, that we're going to turn Brian's life into a quiz. We want you, the audience, to guess the previous job or jobs of our esteemed unlucky guest with the winner receiving a no-expenses-spared, once-in-a-lifetime meal deal from a well known supermarket.

Chorus   Yaay!

Game show host   So, ladies and gentlemen, please give it up for Unlucky Brian!!!!

Chorus   Yaay!

Game show host   Okay, so Brian, give us a clue as to your former job or jobs.

Brian   Well, Mr Showbiz, I sold pick and mix.

Game show host *waits for someone (hopefully) in the audience to say Woolworths, if not a chorus member says it.*

Game show host   Woolworths it is!

Chorus   Yaay!

Game show host   But that's not all is it, Brian? Because after your job at Woolworths, you got another job didn't you?

Brian   Yes, Mr Showbiz, that's right.

Game show host   So, give us a clue as to your second job.

Brian   It's a three letter place where I sold music, CDs, tapes and vinyl.

Game show host   Come on audience, come on, going to have to hurry you . . .

Game show host *waits for someone* (*hopefully*) *in the audience to say HMV, if not a chorus member says it.*

Game show host   HMV! Excellent, excellent.

Chorus   Yaay!

Game show host   But that's not all, as we said, Brian is known as Unlucky Brian, and this job lasted less than a year didn't it, Brian? So give us a clue as to your third job, Brian.

Brian   I rented out videos and DVDs for people to take home and watch in the comfort of their own living rooms.

Game show host *waits for someone* (*hopefully*) *in the audience to say Blockbuster, if not a chorus member says it.*

Game show host   Blockbuster exactly! Remember that one Mrs?

Chorus   Yaay!

Game show host   Well, I don't think anyone in the audience won this week, so that meal deal rolls over till the next programme – let's hope the sandwich doesn't go stale. But poor old Unlucky Brian eh? What a shame, what a jinx? I don't think anybody would dare employ you now, not at the rate you close businesses eh Brian? But thanks for coming onto our show and you don't leave empty handed – unlike the jobs you've had (*'Audience' laughs.*)

– Our lovely assistant has an all expenses paid token for a food bank of your choice.

Lovely Assistant 1 *gives him a big voucher for a food bank. Much cheering and whooping from* **Chorus**.

Game show host   And now, you may remember our lovely stay at home housewife and mother from a previous show. Well. . . . What's your name love?

Natalie's mum   Natalie's mum.

Game show host   Lovely name, lovely name. Well, we invited Natalie's mum to return and have another shot at Get A Job! . . . because she believes she's better than her last job.

Natalie's mum   Erm . . . No I just thought. . . .

Game show host   She thinks she's above her station . . .

Natalie mum   No . . . I didn't say that . . . Er. . . .

Game show host   Being a cleaner's not good enough for our Natalie's mum.

Well let's hope she's right because tonight she's going for gold! She's going for the big one! She's going for ASPIRATION!!!

Chorus   Yaaaay!!!

Game show host   Okay, alright, nice and quiet in the studio. Let's give Natalie's mum a chance to concentrate . . . Okay, Natalie's mum you have sixty seconds to get all the answers written on my card, okay? There are six answers, that's all you've got to get, just six. You can do this, you can do this, we have every faith – (*To audience.*) what do we have?

Chorus   Every faith!!!

Game show host   Okay, all right. Now Natalie's mum. . . . Are you ready?

Natalie's mum   Yes, Mr Showbiz, I'm ready.

Game show host   Okay. For a better job, for aspiration and to work for a better future . . . (*Reading from card.*) . . . What makes you think you have the right to a decent job?

Natalie's mum   Ummm.

Game show host   Come on, have to hurry you . . .

Natalie's mum   Because I work hard and I . . . erm (*Buzzer.*)

Game show host   No, that's not right. Times ticking away . . .

Natalie's mum   I've got kids and (*Buzzer.*) . . . an elderly parent to provide for and (*Buzzer.*) . . . erm. . . . I'm a single parent (*Buzzer.*) . . . er . . .

Game show host   No, come on think, Natalie's mum, think!

Natalie's mum   I voted for the prime minister. (*Ping!*) I'm willing to take any job (*Ping!*) I won't complain about substandard working conditions. (*Ping!*) I won't join a union. (*Ping!*) I was born here (*Ping!*) and . . .

Game show host   Come on, come on . . . one more . . .

Natalie's mum   erm . . . er . . . Oh! Ooh! I'm a hard working family! (*Ping! Ping! Ping! Ping! Ping!*)

Game show host   You've done it! You've done it! Natalie's mum. You. Have. Got. A. Job!

Game show host *raises* **Natalie's mum's** *arm like a prize fighter.*

Dennis's mum   I worked so hard to hold it together. Put my life into the business. I've had to cut half my workforce. Loyal workers, hard workers – redundant. Downsizing, sounds such a nice word but some people have been with me for years.

Dennis   Mum?

Dennis's mum   Not now Dennis I'm failing.

Music: O'Jays – Money, Money, Money, Money.

Natalie's mum   I got a job! I got a job! (*Excited and panicky.*) I start Monday. We'll have to be careful now, for a while, till we get sorted. I'm going to have to buy some clothes, I can't work in tat, can't wear the same clothes over and over like I do at home or when I was cleaning. When we're more settled, more in the rhythm, I might be able to save a bit – it doesn't pay much, minimum wage, and if I lose all my benefits things will be tight, especially, like I say, having to buy more clothes for work. And shoes! I need shoes, these have got holes in and they're falling apart, I can't just stuff them with newspaper when it rains, can I? I can't do that at work. I can't squelch around all day in soaking shoes. And tights! I'm going to have to have a month's supply of tights!

Natalie   Mum?

Natalie's mum   Not now Natalie I'm succeeding.

Game Show Host   A typical day – On your marks, get set, Work!

Music: Dire Straits – Industrial Disease.

Similar to start but slower and more depressed. Everybody getting ready for work, school etc. **Natalie***'s family moving quicker, more frantic. A couple of people lazing around. Some playing parents, kids, some single, childless, again showing the difference and/or similarity in day starts, but definitely much more subdued. A few finishing before others and some standing engrossed in mobile devices.*

Dennis   How's your mum?

Natalie   I don't know, hardly ever see her, and when I do it's just a quick dinner shoved in the oven and pegged out in front of the telly, with her falling asleep. How about yours?

Dennis   Same, except she eats when I'm in bed – at least I assume she does.

Natalie   You eat alone?

Dennis   Most days. Cool phone by the way.

Natalie   Thanks.

Dennis   At least you've got money now.

Natalie   No we haven't, the government has to top up her wages, so we're still on benefits.

Dennis   But your mum's working.

Natalie   Not everyone who works is a millionaire, Dennis. If anything we're worse off now.

Dennis   But you've got a new phone.

Natalie   Grandad bought it for my birthday.

Natalie *waves her phone at* **Grandad**, **Grandad** *waves back.*

Dennis's mum   What do you want for your birthday, Dennis?

Dennis   I'd like you to come and see me in the school play.

Dennis's mum   I'll see what I can do. But, isn't there anything else you'd like?

Dennis *shrugs and goes back to his phone.*

N Friend 1   You say, 'Things are mad at the moment but all this is for later, it'll all come together later.'

N Friend 2   You say, 'Yes I know I'm busy and I've broken a lot of promises and we hardly see each other but soon it will be better.'

N Friend 3   You say, 'This is all for the best, we'll have a good time soon. We're working for the good times.'

N Friend 4   You say, 'We're working for a holiday. We're working for Christmas.'

N Friend 5   You say, 'We will be a family on holiday. We'll be a family at Christmas. We will all be happy on holiday.'

Dennis   Until then we're separate, strangers, loners,

Grandad   lost.

(D Friend 1) George   We're going on holiday.

Natalie   That's fantastic.

George   No it isn't. It happens every year:

D Friends 2–5.   The Nightmare!

Music: Benny Hill Theme (Yakety Sax).

The Nightmare. Everybody desperately and hurriedly scanning devices and maps and magazines, yelling out suggestions:

D Friend 2   Turkey?

D Friend 3   The Azores?

D Friend 4   Disneyland?

D Friend 5   Spain?

George and DF2–5   Spain.

Frenziedly alternating between devices and shopping and planning and packing and preparing for holiday. Clothes, bags, buckets spades etc. flying, everyone racing back and forth, shouting:

D Friend 2   Passport! Euros!

D Friend 3   Where's my swimming costume?

D Friend 4   What shall we do with the dog?

D Friend 5   Anybody got a phrasebook! What language do they speak?

Mad dash for airport, luggage, tickets, trolleys etc. yelling:

D Friend 2   Did you lock the door?

D Friend 3   Have you got the tickets?

D Friend 4   Who's got the plastic bag thingy for the 100ml stuff!

D Friend 5   What happened to the dog?

Arriving. Queuing. Check in. queuing, security. Queuing. Belts, shoes, coats, money in trays. Queuing. Beeping and pat down. Queuing. Checking departure board. Running. Queuing. Plane, queuing. overhead lockers, pushing, shoving, squeezing, sitting, safety drill, standing, overhead lockers, queuing. Shouting out accordingly.

D Friend 2   Check in!

D Friend 3   Departures!

D Friend 4   Security!

hotel

D Friend 5   Swimming pool! No loungers. What's German for 'move your towel'?

D Friend 2   Balcony! No view, I can't see the sea.

D Friend 3   I can't even see the swimming pool. Where's the sun?!

D Friend 4   It's too hot. I hate the food. I can't understand the language.

D Friend 2   And the parents are asleep.

D Friend 3   Or reading.

D Friend 4   I miss the dog.

D Friend 5   And I forgot to pack my Gameboy!

Lily (N Friend 1)   Still sounds more fun than our holidays.

George   What are your holidays like, Lily?

Lily   'Hey kids, fancy going to Wales? . . . Pack your macs then.'

N Friend 2   We go to Ireland every summer and stay with relatives.

N Friend 3   We went to all the different parks around the city one year, it was really good.

N Friend 4   We just do day trips, the seaside, a picnic, boat on a lake, barbeque in the garden, that sort of thing.

N Friend 5   I go and stay with my grandparents.

D Friend 2   I stay with my grandparents too. In the Caymans.

N Friend 5   Mine are in Wigan.

Music: Pink Floyd – Money.

Natalie's mum *in the workplace, with other workers. Doing something repetitive and dull, robotic, but clearly doing it for the* **Boss**. *Possibly passing around the 'pound coins', or something equally passable, ending up on a pile for the* **Boss**. *So that a worker has one to pass and the* **Boss** *has a pile.*

Dennis's mum *is off to one side, not part of the workers scene, so in a different work space.*

Dennis's mum   (*music fades to underscore*) I'm doing this for my family. Or am I doing this for myself? Not now Dennis I'm building up the business. Not now Dennis I'm trying to maintain the business. Not now Dennis the business is failing. Not now Dennis the business has failed. I want to be fair. I tried to be fair, but somewhere along the line, we all changed. It started being dog eat dog, every man for him or herself. And I hate it but I have to compete. I employed thousands of people, now there's only a few hundred but I still believe I give them decent working conditions, and I still believe I give them decent wages. I don't want to be the enemy. I don't believe I am. I am just trying to be successful . . . But . . . is it success if I can't see Dennis in his play? (*Music builds and stops.*)

Union Rep   Hang on, hang on, hang on, Comrades, do I detect a whiff of worker exploitation?

Boss   No, we need the profits to build up the business.

Union Rep   Without the workers there would be no business.

Boss   It's *my* business.

Union Rep   Which you can't grow without us.

Boss   I don't need the unions.

Union Rep   But we do. Without the unions . . .

Every other worker puts their coin or similar onto the boss's pile. Then, with partner who still has their coin or similar, an exchange of looks, envy, trying to get the coin, escalating into a tussle, then all out riot/fight amongst the workers.

Union Rep   Comrades, comrades, simmer down. Come on, calm yourselves.

But *with* the unions. . . .

The workers take two coins or similar from the bosses pile, so that the **Boss** *has less, but still more than the workers.*

Boss   I have to say I preferred it the other way.

Union Rep   But slow growth is better than no growth. Or you could try doing it *all* on your own.

The group disperse. **Union Rep** *pays* **Natalie's mum** *a coin or similar. She is left behind with the* **Boss**.

Boss   I see you've got your wages.

Natalie's mum   Yes . . . thank you.

Boss   Could you just take them to that person (*The* **Politician**.) over there?

Natalie's mum   What?

Boss   Your wages go from me to them. All you are is the carrier.

Natalie's mum   But I earned that money.

Boss   Yes, you did, you earned the right to hold it for a moment. But unless you are very rich you don't get to keep it. You merely pass it from one rich person to the next – And in some circumstances you end up owing us money. Funny I know but it happens more often than you'd think.

Music: Pink Floyd – Money (Instrumental Reprise).

Natalie   Got any biscuits, Mum?

Natalie's mum   (*tiredly*) In the shopping bag, Natalie.

Miranda   I want to talk but they say 'I'm tired'

David   They say 'Isn't it time for bed?'

Fishing Boy   They say 'Have you done your homework?'

Maths Boy   They say 'Have you got everything ready for school in the morning?'

Boarding School Girl   I want to talk, I want to say, 'Do you see me?' 'Do you hear me?'

Timetable Girl   I want to say, 'Can we talk?'

Kids in Chorus

- They say 'It's time for bed,'
- 'It's late'
- 'It's time for tea'
- 'Time for supper'
- 'Time for dinner'
- 'It's late'
- 'We're late'
- 'It's time for school'
- 'You're late'
- 'It's late'
- 'I'm late'
- 'We're late'
- 'You're late'
- 'They're late'

Grandad   It's too late.

A&E Worker   If I don't work I can't afford the rent.

Postman   Can't afford the mortgage.

Banker   Can't afford childcare.

Boss   Can't afford the car.

Dog Shelter Volunteer   Can't afford a holiday.

Gas board Worker   Can't afford food.

Union Rep   Or clothes.

Parents in Chorus   (*some on devices*)

- If I worked less hours the commute costs the same and I couldn't afford to even get to work.
- I've got to pay for carers to keep an eye on my mum, she's getting old and she's not always capable.
- Extra tuition fees just to get them to university, give them a good start.
- All I want is two weeks sunshine, just to stop for two weeks, recharge my batteries and feel the sun on my skin.
- To just sit and relax and not be thinking 'What needs doing?' 'What can I get done?'
- I do all my shopping on my iPad, while I'm sitting on the train.
- Google maps, where would I be without Google maps? Lost that's where I'd be.
- Online banking, I pay all my bills, sort out all my money worries while I'm waiting for the bus.

Kids in Chorus   (*some on devices*)

- I play Candy Crush.
- I'm on World of Warcraft.
- My sister lols and omg's on Facebook, Snapchat and Tinder.
- My brother digs on Minecraft.
- I am living in Sim.

Parents in Chorus   (*all speakers on devices*)

- Sometimes I pretend I'm watching TV with the kids but I'm actually internet shopping – I couldn't get it done otherwise.
- They don't notice, I just laugh when they laugh,
- they think I'm watching.

Politician   Hard working families . . .

Grandad   What is your definition of hard working families?

PS   People who do a decent day's work.

PA   For a decent day's pay.

Grandad   Most people are doing the decent day's work but not getting the decent day's pay and not getting the decent day's rest.

Parents from Cast & Chorus   (*more on devices*)

- Who's looking after my kids?
- How are they being brought up?
- What are they doing?
- Where are they going?
- When will we be a proper family?
- What are they eating?
- Who are they mixing with?

Kids from Cast & Chorus   (*more on devices*)

- I'm being bullied.
- I've got toothache.
- I think I need glasses I can't see the board.
- I don't know how to do maths and the teacher hasn't got time to explain it.
- I just want someone to explain it, to help me.
- I've got tummy ache.
- The girls at school don't like me.

Parents from Cast & Chorus

- *everybody's life is better than mine*
- *everybody else's kids are blessed*
- *everybody else knows the secret of success*
- *nobody else feels so depressed*

Kids from Cast & Chorus   (*more on devices*)

- I haven't any friends.
- School's too big and I feel too small.
- I'm scared.
- I'm lonely.
- I don't understand.
- I've got no one to play with.
- My friend is no longer my friend.
- I need help.
- I need someone to talk to.
- I need reassurance.
- I need confidence.

All parents   I just need five minutes. (*more on devices*)

Miranda   Watch me Mummy.

David   Watch me Daddy.

All kids   Why won't you just watch me?

Parents from Cast & Chorus   (*more on devices*)

– *everybody else is making ends meet*
– *everybody else isn't failing*
– *everybody else isn't rushed off their feet*
– *nobody else is complaining.*
– I'm self employed
– I'm clinging on
– I can't pay the mortgage
– I can't pay the rent
– It's almost against the law to enjoy my job
– To enjoy my family
– To enjoy my life.

Dennis   (*on a device, but looking up to speak*) I have everything. Surrounded by things. Surrounded by stuff. I can't think of anything I want. Except for my mum to see me. I want her to see me in the school play. I know she won't come, can't come. There are things more important.

Natalie   (*on a device, but looking up to speak*) More important than you?

Dennis   Yes. Money. Money's more important. She wants to give me wealth, she wants to give me health, she wants to buy my happiness. But I just want her. Money is above me, money comes before me, it is worth more than me, I am worth less.

Both go back to devices.

Grandad   In the 70s the derogatory term was 'latchkey kids'. Thoughtless selfish women going out to work when they should have been at home. Now the derogatory term is 'stay at home mum'. Thoughtless selfish women not going out to work.

All   (*most on devices, looking up to speak*)

Money is above me,
money comes before me,
it is worth more than me,
I am worth less.

Parents from Cast & Chorus   (*most on devices, looking up to speak*)

We're just ticking over, just getting by
Trying to save for a mortgage
Rents have gone sky high
We're just ticking over, putting up with that
I'm living with my mum and dad
I can't afford a flat
We're stretched to the limit, belts are tightened tight
We're counting pennies daily
And dreaming of pounds at night

Banker   I used to garden but it's all overgrown now, it's such a mess – but I don't have the time. (*On a device.*)

Dog Shelter Volunteer   I just buy all my clothes now, and my husband's shirts and kids' clothes, I used to like to sew but . . . I haven't got the time and I'm exhausted in the evenings. (*On a device.*)

Gas Board Worker   Can't afford to run the car anymore, price of petrol – anyway I've started working weekends just to make ends meet, so haven't got time to drive. (*On a device.*)

Grandad   In the beginning men worked and women stayed at home. But the times changed. Life's not the same. Women's work changed but men's didn't.

A&E Worker   I am perfectly capable of doing a man's job but I can't do a man's job and a woman's job as well. (*On a device.*)

Postman   I am perfectly capable of doing a woman's job but I can't do a woman's job and a man's job as well. (*On a device.*)

Boss   I haven't got a nanny. I can't afford an au pair. Child minders cost a fortune. The nursery is full. I just can't afford it. I want to stop juggling. I want to stop running around like a headless chicken. I want to stop the stress. I want to see my child. I want to be with my children, is that a crime? (*On a device.*)

By now everyone, except **Grandad**, *has their face illuminated by their devices.*

Grandad   In my parents' day, men worked and women stayed at home. Most could afford the rent or the mortgage. Now both men and women work and few can afford the rent or the mortgage. It's a funny old world.

Kids from Cast & Chorus

– How much does it cost to spend time with my family?
– How much cut in pay if you saw me in the school play?
– Would the economy collapse if I got ill on a weekday?
– Would the world stop if we had a family life?

Grandad   Grandma said four hours. The majority should only work four hours, both men and women, especially parents. Mind you Grandma was an anarchist.

Politician   Due to the deficit, the recession and a stagnant economy, we have to make sacrifices and tighten our belts.

PS   Cut, cut

PA   and cut again

Politician   – it's the only road to recovery. Pay will be frozen and prices increase. Unemployment statistics must come down.

PS   Everyone has to work,

PA   everybody has to get a job.

Politician   We can no longer carry people who aren't prepared to contribute. We are all in it together

PS   and we must freeze some benefits

PA   and withdraw others.

Politician   At the same time we are going to kick-start the economy and stimulate recovery by a few strategic tax cuts.

A huge giant 'AAAAAgggghhhhh' from everybody. Lights off on devices – back to reality.

Natalie's mum   No. No. I've had enough. You're driving me away from my family. You're making me work against my family. Hard work is not rewarded because women's work is hard work and I've already got a job. I'm a mum!

Dennis's mum   (*to* **Politician**) Have you ever seen your son in the school play?

(**Politician** *goes to say 'yes'.*)

Dennis's mum   When the cameras weren't there?

(**Politician** *changes his/her mind and shakes head sadly 'no'.*)

Dennis's mum   I'm going to see my son.

Politician   Let me just explain, you see if you vote for me . . .

Natalie's mum   No, I've had enough of listening to you. I'm listening to me and I'm making biscuits.

Dennis's mum   Can I try one?

Natalie's mum   It'll cost you.

Dennis's mum   Now you're talking my language.

Natalie   Yes, Mum you could sell them! Bespoke organic artisan hand made individually prepared natural ingredients home made taste the goodness half fat full flavour double chock double chip biscuits.

Dennis's mum   The aspirational will love them.

Natalie's mum   Now, Natalie, you're talking my language.

Dennis   You could make a fortune.

Dennis's mum   (*to* **Natalie's mum**) Let's do lunch.

Music: Florence & The Machine – Dog Days Are Over (or similar trending, up beat, galvanising song.)